Web Business Engineering

Addison-Wesley Information Technology Series

Capers Jones and David S. Linthicum, Consulting Editors

The information technology (IT) industry is in the public eye now more than ever before because of a number of major issues in which software technology and national policies are closely related. As the use of software expands, there is a continuing need for business and software professionals to stay current with the state of the art in software methodologies and technologies. The goal of the Addison-Wesley Information Technology Series is to cover any and all topics that affect the IT community: These books illustrate and explore how information technology can be aligned with business practices to achieve business goals and support business imperatives. Addison-Wesley has created this innovative series to empower you with the benefits of the industry experts' experience.

For more information point your browser to
http://www.awl.com/cseng/series/it/

Sid Adelman, Larissa Terpeluk Moss, *Data Warehouse Project Management*. ISBN: 0201616351

Wayne Applehans, Alden Globe, and Greg Laugero, *Managing Knowledge: A Practical Web-Based Approach*. ISBN: 0-201-43315-X

Michael H. Brackett, Data Resource Quality: Turning Bad Habits into Good Practices. ISBN: 0201713063

Gregory C. Dennis and James R. Rubin, *Mission-Critical Java™ Project Management: Business Strategies, Applications, and Development*. ISBN: 0-201-32573-X

Kevin Dick, *XML: A Manager's Guide*. ISBN: 0-201-43335-4

Jill Dyché, *e-Data: Turning Data into Information with Data Warehousing*. ISBN: 0-201-65780-5

Dr. Nick V. Flor, *Web Business Engineering: Using Offline Activites to Drive Internet Strategies*. ISBN: 020160468X

David Garmus and David Herron, *Function Point Analysis: Measurement Practices for Successful Software Projects*. ISBN: 0201699443

Capers Jones, *Software Assessments, Benchmarks, and Best Practices*. ISBN: 0-201-48542-7

Capers Jones, *The Year 2000 Software Problem: Quantifying the Costs and Assessing the Consequences*. ISBN: 0-201-30964-5

Ravi Kalakota and Marcia Robinson, *e-Business: Roadmap for Success*. ISBN: 0-201-60480-9

David S. Linthicum, *Enterprise Application Integration*. ISBN: 0-201-61583-5

Sergio Lozinsky, *Enterprise-Wide Software Solutions: Integration Strategies and Practices*. ISBN: 0-201-30971-8

Patrick O'Beirne, *Managing the Euro in Information Systems: Strategies for Successful Changeover*. ISBN: 0-201-60482-5

Mai-lan Tomsen, *Killer Content: Strategies for Web Content and E-Commerce*. ISBN: 0-201-65786-4

Bill Wiley, *Essential System Requirements: A Practical Guide to Event-Driven Methods*. ISBN: 0-201-61606-8

Bill Zoellick, *Web Engagement: Connecting to Customers in e-Business*. ISBN: 0-201-65766-X

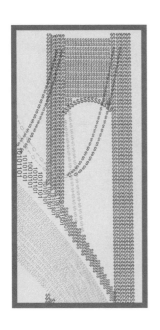

Web Business Engineering

Using Offline Activities
to Drive Internet
Strategies

Nick V. Flor

Addison-Wesley

Boston • San Francisco • New York • Toronto • Montreal
London • Munich • Paris • Madrid
Capetown • Sydney • Tokyo • Singapore • Mexico City

The publisher offers discounts on this book when ordered in quantity for special sales. For more information, please contact:

Pearson Education Corporate Sales Division
One Lake Street
Upper Saddle River, NJ 07458
(800) 382-3419
corpsales@pearsontechgroup.com

Visit AW on the Web: www.awl.com/cseng/

Library of Congress Cataloging-in-Publication Data

Flor, Nick V.
      Web business engineering : using offline activities to drive
Internet strategies / by Nick V. Flor.
            p.   cm.
      Includes bibliographical references and index.
      ISBN 0-201-60468-X (alk. paper)
            1. Electronic commerce—Planning.   2. Web sites—Design.
3. Internet.   I. Title.
      HF5548.32 F58 2000
      658.8'00285'4678—dc21   00-058277

ISBN 0-201-60468-X
Text printed on recycled paper
1 2 3 4 5 6 7 8 9 10-MA-04 03 02 01 00
First printing, October 2000

For Nancy, Pete, and Mikki

Contents

CHAPTER 11 WBE IN LARGE INSTITUTIONS: THE ONLINE SURVEY CASE   127

CHAPTER 12 WBE IN SOCIAL/CULTURAL SITUATIONS: THE CASE OF THE ONLINE MATCHMAKING SERVICE   141

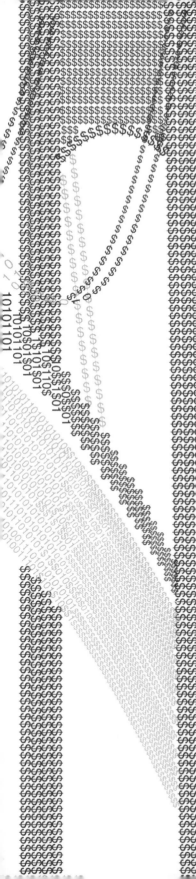

Preface

*The idea is not to get as complicated as you
can, but to get as much of yourself into it as
you can. Music has to go places.*
                                    —Jimi Hendrix

In the fall of 1994, I was hired as a faculty member at
Carnegie Mellon University's Business School—the Graduate School of Industrial Administration (GSIA). Because the
Web was still in its infancy at that time, there were no courses
at GSIA, or at any other top business school, that taught
systematic methods for effectively using the Web in businesses. So I decided that I would teach such a course. I ran
this idea past some of my more senior colleagues, who were
less than enthusiastic. A common remark was "The Web is
just a fad. It's not going anywhere. We've had the Internet for
years." However, having worked as an engineer on the Web's
predecessor (Time Warner's Interactive-TV project)—not to
mention doing a multiuser Internet adventure game (MUD)
as part of my thesis research—I knew the Web was an important technology with potentially far-reaching implications
for both consumers and businesses. I therefore set out to
create such a course. A year later, I received a grant from the
government (DARPA) through Stanford University's Enterprise Integration Technologies program for my Virtual
Market Square project. The goal of this project was to train
businesses on how to properly use the Web and other Internet technologies. This book is the culmination of four years
of research and teaching on the general topic of how to use
online technologies effectively in businesses.

I think you will find this book very different from other
technical Web or business books you may have read. It is

neither a purely technical book that details the latest online technology (such as Dynamic HTML), nor is it purely a business book that examines several cases of successful Web companies (such as Amazon.com) to present a set of best management practices. The Web as we currently know it is a collection of technologies in flux. As the technologies underlying the Web change, the nature of competition also shifts, so today's successful Web companies may not be successful tomorrow. One need only look at Netscape for an example of how quickly a successful Web company can fall.

Don't get me wrong. I'm not arguing against studying Web technological details or case studies of successful Web companies. Both can provide insights into what a company should be doing on the Web. What I do argue, however, is that a company's most effective strategy for using the Web is typically not found by copying what successful "online" companies are doing but rather by careful analysis of *what successful companies are doing offline.* The emphasis is not on what successful online companies are doing now but rather on what companies ought to be doing online based on their "offline" activities.

The Web strategy I advocate in this book can be summed up with the following statement: ***Use offline activities to drive online activities.*** In short, the activities that a company is doing offline should determine what activities that company does online. If you are a Web entrepreneur thinking of starting your own Web company, the strategy still holds, except you use the offline activities of successful *existing* companies to drive what you do online. In this manner, business constrains technology, not vice versa. The key is to have some kind of method for effectively analyzing offline activities. This book provides you a systematic method for doing such an analysis.

In closing, I believe the real business uses of the Web have yet to be discovered. This book can help you map out those uses.

Acknowledgments

In writing this book, I've benefited tremendously from the support of my family, friends, and students. In particular I'd like to acknowledge my wife, Nancy, who forced me to stop noodling around on my guitar and finish this book (she also bought me many good "toys" to keep my motivation high). My sister Judy and her husband, Hugo Kostelni, gave me several important ideas for the chapter on valuing your Web site. Several friends also deserve mention: Paul Maglio, who helped me develop and write the material in the first case study, which is derived from an academic article we published jointly; the gang at the 61C Coffee Shop, who provided me with coffee and an electrical outlet for my laptop; and Amy Goulet, who helped with the Dating Expert material. My students, both graduate and undergraduate, deserve mention for testing and validating the theories and techniques in this book. I'd also like to thank my editors, Elizabeth Spainhour, Mariann Kourafas, Jacquelyn Doucette, and Mary O'Brien, who kept me on schedule, and the many reviewers who provided important comments on how to improve the material in this book. Finally, I'd like to thank my dear parents, Nemesiano and Balbina Flor, just for being themselves.

Introduction

From a business perspective, the Web is a technology *in search of* a business need instead of a technology *serving* a business need. True, there are millions of businesses with Web sites distributed across the world. But the huge number of existing sites does not mean that businesses have discovered how to effectively use the Web. Indeed, many of the early high-profile Web pioneers who were touted as leading the Web revolution are either losing money, shutting down, or filing for bankruptcy.

- Microsoft closed half the Web sites it created last year, fired several hundred part-time employees, announced the termination of ten programs on its Microsoft Network, and was reported to be considering getting out of the Internet service provider business altogether.
- CompuServe, an online pioneer, announced financial losses, the resignation of its chief executive officer, and a shift from the mass consumer market to business and professional users.
- Time Warner was said to be losing as much as $10 million a year on *Pathfinder.com*, the Internet site that features *Time, People, Money,* and other Time Inc. magazines. (Dan Logan, chief executive officer of Time Inc., has described Pathfinder as giving a "new definition to the term 'black hole.'")

- Politics Now, a popular World Wide Web site run by ABC News, the *Washington Post,* and the *National Journal,* closed down. So did such Internet magazines as *Out* and *Spiv* and an online Web directory called Netguide Live and the Web soap opera *The Spot,* which had been hailed as a prototype for Internet entertainment. American Cybercast, producer of *The Spot,* has filed for bankruptcy protection.

In short, the large number of current Web sites merely indicates the ease with which information can be put online. But there is an important difference between creating *a* Web site and creating a *business* Web site. A Web site exchanges *information,* whereas a business Web site exchanges *value*—that is, it generates significant revenues or drastically cuts costs in a business. And the basic problem is that we do not really know how to design high-value Web sites. We can easily develop "any old" Web site but not a business Web site. Web strategy books follow this formula: (1) present a platitude, (2) present many examples of businesses that seem to support that platitude, (3) conclude that the reader's business should do the same. I believe that every company is its own gold mine of Web strategic ideas. This book teaches you how to mine for these ideas.

This book teaches both Web consultants and Web entrepreneurs how to systematically develop a business Web site, or what I simply call *Web Business Engineering.* The key word here is *systematically.* While it's certainly possible for one to get lucky and create a high-value Web site without Web Business Engineering, it's not worth the risk, especially if you are a consultant or entrepreneur who stands to lose clients or significant profits from an ineffective site. By using Web Business Engineering you have a much better chance of developing a high-value, business Web site. My technique combines business concepts with engineering-strength design and analysis techniques to form a methodology that Web consultants and entrepreneurs alike can use to create business Web sites.

If you don't know a thing about business or engineering, don't worry. I wrote this book with the assumption that you, the reader, know absolutely nothing about either subject. Indeed, I started out teaching Web Business Engineering to second-year undergraduate business students and first-year MBAs, neither of which were particularly sophisticated (yet) in either business or analysis and design. However, if you do have a strong technical or business background, you'll find that the material covered in my book complements your existing skills. Technical types should find my book's treatment of business topics a necessary supplement to their "hard" skills, and business types will discover that the business analysis parts of Web Business Engineering allow them to better apply their experience toward solving online business problems.

Before we begin, let's try to understand why it's difficult to develop a *business* Web site (remember, we're talking about business Web sites, not just any Web site). Knowing why will put us in a better position to identify the skills we need to create them. I will start off examining why it's difficult for individuals to design business Web sites and then identify the key skills needed to design high-value Web sites. Finally, I will describe the organization of this book and how it helps you acquire these skills.

Why Developing Business Web Sites Is Difficult

It should come as no surprise that people have a difficult time discovering the most effective business uses of the Web. Whenever a radically new technology like the Web emerges, both the designers of the technology and its users typically have a hard time determining its most effective application. Ways of using a technology that seem obvious to future users are difficult to envision when the technology first appears. For example, when the telephone first came out, it was difficult for people to imagine using it for social calls; the telephone was only supposed to be used for emergencies! The radio is another example. Record companies originally thought that playing songs on the radio would destroy record sales. It seemed obvious that consumers would not buy records, since they could hear the songs on the radio for free. Of course, we now know that the radio and record player (CD players nowadays!) are complementary technologies that benefit one another. These are not unique incidents. History is full of examples that suggest the most effective use of any radical new technology is difficult to discover. The question is, Why?

The answer can be found by understanding that "no technology is an island." Any new technology is ultimately destined to become part of a larger, more complex social and technological organization, which can range from homes to large firms to entire cultures. Understanding the best use of a technology requires that one understand both the technology and the organization in which it is embedded. Unfortunately, most people focus on the technology's properties and not the organization's processes. This can lead to ineffective uses of new technology, especially when the technology is multifaceted. If one focuses on the wrong properties, or features, of the technology, then its initial application will center on those features, even though the technology may be best used for other applications.

The Web is a perfect example of such a multifaceted new technology. Its most salient feature is its ability to serve up pages of information. Thus, initial organizational use of the Web revolved around placing paper-based information online. Indeed, the bulk of the initial wave of corporate Web sites were nothing more than online versions of paper-based, corporate brochures. Companies would convert their brochures, catalogs, manuals, and almost anything else that they had on paper into Web pages. However, application of the Web as "electronic paper" is inefficient because it totally underutilizes the Web's computational, storage, and networking capabilities. Even today, companies still struggle with finding good interactive applications of the Web that truly exploit its computational capabilities. In fact, one can still find many Web sites that are nothing more than static, online brochures.

To effectively use the Web, one needs to understand not just the Web's properties but also, and more importantly, the activities or processes of whatever organization will use it. This organizational-centered approach to the Web creates Web sites that support and augment existing business processes, thus— almost by definition—adding value to the organization that uses it. In this book, the organization of interest is a business. So, we need systematic methods that help us discover how to mold the Web to the specific requirements of different kinds of businesses. Without such methods, businesses may have to stumble around for a while until they "evolve" a high-value Web site through trial and error. Unfortunately, in today's fast-paced, highly competitive marketplace, such a slow, evolutionary approach toward the Web can be disastrous!

What We Need to Know to Develop Business Web Sites

I hope I've convinced you of the importance of understanding both the Web's technical capabilities (technological properties) and the business activities (organizational or business processes) of whatever firm intends to use it. For Web business consultants, this is a client's firm, and for Web business entrepreneurs, the firm is their own. There's a plethora of printed and online material available to help you understand the Web's technical details. My job is to teach you how to understand business activities so that you can adapt the Web to your processes, instead of the converse. In my organizational-centered approach to designing business Web sites, the Web becomes a technology that *serves* business needs, not a technology *in search of* a business need.

The business-centered approach to designing high-value Web sites requires that you have the following skills:

1. *General business knowledge.* You need to know how a business works from the formulation of an idea to the realization of that idea as a product, as well as the marketing and supporting of the product. For Web entrepreneurs, this knowledge can help you decide what kind of Web business to start. For Web consultants, this knowledge can help you communicate better with clients as well as give you a broad sense of where to apply Web technologies most effectively in a business.

2. *The ability to analyze and diagnose specific businesses activities.* Businesses, even those in the same industry, can be very different in terms of how they're run, which is a function of the technology they use, employee makeup, and corporate culture, to name a few. So, you need more than just general business knowledge to find the best uses of the Web. Web consultants and entrepreneurs need techniques to help them diagnose specific businesses for the purpose of discovering areas where the Web can best be applied. Web consultants will apply these diagnosis skills toward analyzing clients' businesses and looking for opportunities to cut costs or generate revenues. Similarly, Web entrepreneurs will apply their diagnosis skills toward analyzing existing businesses or industries with the goal of identifying new business ventures.

3. *The ability to design "Web treatments" for specific business problems or opportunities.* Being aware of a problem or knowing about an area of opportunity is not the same thing as having a solution for it. Once you've identified specific areas in a business or industry that could benefit from the Web, the next step is designing "Web treatments" for those areas. In the context of Web Business Engineering, a Web treatment is defined simply as a use of the Web that supports or extends a business process or set of business processes. A treatment can range from a mere design of added content for a client's Web site, which is what a Web consultant typically does, to the design of an entire Web site, in the case of a Web entrepreneur.

What's interesting is that as a Web business engineer your primary role is neither business manager nor engineer but one of a physician of sorts. But whereas a doctor treats people, you treat businesses; you diagnose a business or industry, looking for problems or opportunities, and you design treatments. The medicine you prescribe to fix a firm's problems or to take advantage of its opportunities is the Web. This book presents a method I developed as part of my research and teaching at Carnegie Mellon University's Graduate School of Industrial Administration. Both my students and I have applied and refined the method over the past four years both as Web consultants helping businesses find their best use of the Web and also as Web entrepreneurs creating profitable online businesses.

Book Outline

This book is organized as follows. Section 1: Web Business 101 covers the first key skill—general business knowledge. Section 2: Web Business Engineering: A Quick Primer covers diagnosis and treatment skills. Section 3: Case Studies: Putting Offline Activities Online demonstrates the breadth of Web Business Engineering by applying it to several different cases. Section 4: Case Studies: Applying Web Business Engineering to Online Activities teaches you how to apply Web Business Engineering to analyze online activities as well, such as online marketing and revenue generation. I'll describe each section in a little more detail.

Section 1. Web Business 101. This first section provides those prospective Web consultants and Web entrepreneurs without business experience the "big picture" as far as businesses are concerned. Specifically, it examines the various components of a business and how these components fit together to transform ideas and raw materials into products. The section also describes the role market-ing, sales, and support play in delivering products to consumers, as well as the nature of competition and how the Web can give companies a strategic advantage over their competitors. As mentioned earlier, as a Web consultant, this kind of knowledge will help you both communicate more easily with your clients and also to quickly identify various opportunities throughout your clients' entire organization where the Web can be used to generate revenues or cut costs. And for Web entrepreneurs, this knowledge can help you better decide what kind of online business to start.

Section 2. Web Business Engineering: A Quick Primer. Once you under-stand how businesses work in general, you can focus on the problem of discover-ing ways to improve specific businesses through Web Business Engineering. In Web Business Engineering, an analysis of a business's offline activities determines what that business should do online—on the Web. This section provides a primer on Web Business Engineering. The aim is to give you a quick sense of the major steps involved in Web Business Engineering without getting into all the details and special cases, so you can start applying it immediately.

Section 3. Case Studies: Putting Offline Activities Online. You can apply Web Business Engineering to a wide variety of business situations. Section 3 explores three case studies where Web Business Engineering is applied to the problem of designing a business Web site or Web application for an actual business. Specifically, Web Business Engineering is used in a small business and a large institution, and applied to a sociocultural problem.

Section 4. Case Studies: Applying Web Business Engineering to Online Activities. The final section shows you how to apply Web Business Engineering to analyze and improve *online* activities. Three cases are explored. The first looks at how you use Web Business Engineering to generate traffic. The second case applies Web Business Engineering to developing the theoretical foundation for Memetic Marketing: a technique for the rapid and widespread marketing of your Web site's content. The third case applies Web Business to the problem of optimizing revenues for a Web site.

So, without further ado, let's learn Web Business Engineering!

Web Business 101

Chances are that you have a good understanding of the technical aspects of the Web. Such knowledge can be readily applied when either you as a Web entrepreneur or the clients you consult for have a good idea of what they want in a Web site. However, when neither you nor your clients know what kind of Web site is needed, technical knowledge becomes secondary to business knowledge. By understanding how businesses work, you can suggest better and more diverse ways of using the Web to add value to either your own business or a client's business. The aim of this section is to give you an overview of how businesses work, how competition affects businesses, and how to determine the value of a Web site.

CHAPTER ONE

Business Building Blocks

Executive Summary

Creating high-value business Web sites requires that you have business as well as technical knowledge. This chapter discusses some of that key business knowledge in the context of examining how an idea becomes a product. It also describes the role a business and other firms play in creating that product. A framework is provided that you can use to help identify general areas where the Web can be effectively used in either your own or a client's business.

Objectives

After reading this chapter you should be able to:

- *Explain how an idea becomes a product*
- *Describe the key agents in the value chain*
- *Describe the four key areas that can benefit from the Web*

Introduction

As a Web entrepreneur or Web consultant you probably have excellent technical skills. These skills are especially valuable when you or your clients have a good idea of what is needed in the Web site. However, when neither you nor your client knows what kind of Web site to build, technical knowledge is not sufficient; business skills are needed as well. Without business knowledge guiding Web site designs, one typically ends up either (1) creating what amounts to an electronic advertisement/online catalog or (2) finding out who your or your client's competitors are and copying their Web site—that is, if they have one. While there is absolutely nothing wrong with either the simple online brochure and catalog style or the copycat design technique, such sites do not fully exploit the computational and multimedia capabilities of the Web in a manner that provides the most value. (By the way, we'll be using the term *value* quite a bit, so let me give you a practical definition that is sufficient for our purposes: A Web site or Web application has value if it makes money or saves money for either you, as a Web entrepreneur, or your client, when you consult.) Your goal then is to create a site or application that has the most value—to create a high-value-added business Web site.

Part of the reason such sites are difficult to create is that we still tend to think about the Web as something that is largely static. In fact, the language we use to talk about the Web betrays this static mindset. We talk about Web *pages* and *surfing to* sites, instead of Web *instruments* and sites *serving* us content. This attitude prevents us from seeing and exploiting the full power of the Web. In reality, the Web is more than a network of electronic pages; it is more usefully thought of as a network of *computational instruments* that can support a wide variety of business activities beyond merely advertising and purchasing. In fact, any information-based business activity is a potential candidate for Web support.

Okay, so let's assume that you do buy into the idea that the Web is a collection of (networked) computational instruments and not pages. There is still the problem of designing Web instruments that provide high value for businesses. An important part of the solution to this problem is business knowledge. Business knowledge, by itself, gives one a broader sense of where and how the Web can most effectively support a client's business or one's own online business. Thus, it's important that you have some business knowledge if you want to create Web sites with high value. However, to get a narrower sense of where to apply the Web most effectively in a business, you also need a technique that allows you to analyze specific business processes—either your client's or competitor's—and derive specific Web applications that support those processes. This is Web Business Engineering.

Together, technical knowledge, business knowledge, and Web Business Engineering provide the tools needed to develop high-value-added Web sites and Web applications. This book assumes you have good technical skills and focuses on augmenting your knowledge with business and Web Business Engineering skills. First, let's focus on business knowledge.

The topic of *businesses* is a complex one. A master's in business administration (MBA) typically takes two years to complete, so it is unreasonable to expect comprehensive coverage in just a couple of chapters. In fact, just giving a list of business terms and their definitions would take up an entire book. For this book's purposes, we'll look at fictitious businesses, how they are created, and how they compete with other businesses. The idea is to give you the big picture, or a "mental model" of how a typical business works. You can then adapt this model to your own or your client's business.

The first fictitious business we examine is a guitar manufacturer. The concepts uncovered in our examination can be easily generalized to other types of businesses because guitar manufacturing is a complex business: (1) a guitar is composed of many different parts, (2) a guitar must be combined with other products to be useful, such as amplifiers and pedals, (3) a guitar requires a considerable amount of knowledge to be played effectively, and (4) there is a community of guitar users. Let's see what it takes to create a "simple" product like a guitar.

How an Idea Becomes a Product: The Case of the Guitar

Imagine you are an electric guitar player. Now suppose that for a number of reasons you aren't satisfied with the guitars currently being sold in music stores. In your not so humble opinion, current guitars neither sound good, play good, nor look good. You think you have a good idea of what a great guitar should be, and you feel that other guitarists also share your views. Okay, at this point, all you have is an idea. How do you make this idea a reality? The short answer is, you create a *business*. A nice, albeit nonstandard, way to think about a business is as a kind of reality generator: The business is the thing that takes your idea and makes it real. Now you probably have something like the picture in Figure 1-1 in mind, but as you'll see, there are many more pieces needed to make your idea real.

Figure 1-1. *The preliminary big picture*

Producer, Consumers, and the Market

Before we go on, let's look at some basic business terms. As a guitar maker, you are also what is commonly known as a *producer.* Anyone who owns a business produces something. That something can be a physical good, like a guitar, or it can be something less tangible, like information (a guitar book or guitar training software), or it can be a *service,* like fixing guitars. The guitarists that buy your guitars are your *consumers.* All the guitarists that could potentially buy your guitars make up your market. Now that you have the big picture, let's set out to make your idea a reality.

The Role of Suppliers

Because you are producing an electric guitar and not an acoustic one, you can't just take the wood in your backyard and start carving it up (and even if you could, you would quickly run out of wood). What you need are suppliers to give you the parts you need for your guitar. Some of these parts are shown in

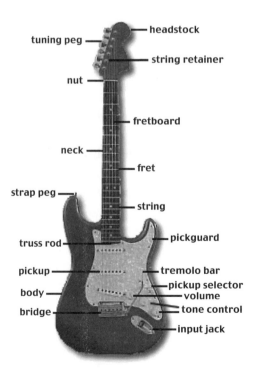

Figure 1-2.   *The main parts of a guitar*

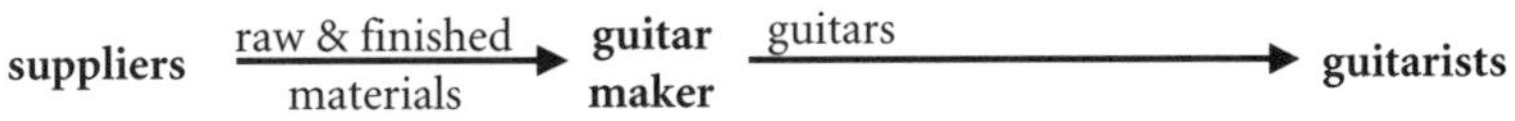

suppliers $\xrightarrow{\text{raw \& finished materials}}$ **guitar maker** $\xrightarrow{\text{guitars}}$ guitarists

Figure 1-3.   *The big picture: how suppliers fit in*

Figure 1-2. There are many other parts that are not shown, such as the electrical components underneath the pick guard, which include resistors, capacitors, potentiometers, wires, and various switches, to name a few.

I should point out that this guitar looks very much like my own except that mine has a large headstock, 22 frets, Custom Shop '69 pickups, and a pearloid pick guard. My point is not to brag about my guitar (well, maybe a little) but to point out that even given these components there is room for considerable variation. It is unrealistic for you to manufacture all the parts. For example, making only the electronics parts required for the volume and control knobs would be a business in itself. Thus, the first decision you have to make as a potential guitar manufacturer is the "make versus buy" decision. As the term implies, this is a decision about which components to manufacture from raw materials (like wood) and which to buy in finished form (like strings, electrical components). In both cases, your company must obtain parts from suppliers. Now in case it isn't apparent, suppliers are simply other businesses that provide the raw materials or finished components that your company uses to make its own products. From the suppliers' perspective, *they* are the producers and *you* are the consumer!

Most small electric guitar makers elect to build just the body and neck of the guitar, while the suppliers provide the other components. A large guitar maker may build the pickups, bridge, strings, nuts, and pick guards as well. Let's assume that you, as a small guitar maker, will only make the body and neck of the guitar. Your big picture is now as seen in Figure 1-3.

The Role of Manufacturing

Okay, you have the supplies. Your next steps are to transform the raw materials into finished materials and then to combine them with the finished supplies to create the finished product. These steps are known as manufacturing. Specifically, manufacturing is that part of your business that molds the raw materials into their finished forms and then assembles the finished components into the final product.

Manufacturing can vary according to how automated your facilities are. For example, you could manually cut and shape the wood into the guitar's neck and body; manually sand, paint, and finish the wood; and manually assemble the finished wood along with the other finished supplies to make a guitar. At the other extreme, you could fully automate your guitar manufacturing. You could use a computer numeric controlled (CNC) machine to cut the wood to within a thousandth of an inch of your specification. You could then automate an entire production line to assemble all the finished components into a finished product: the guitar. Alternatively, you could use a combination of automation and hand-crafting. For example, a CNC machine could cut the wood, but the guitar maker would still sand, paint, and assemble all components by hand. The guitar maker's level of automation is a complex function of how many guitars he or she would like to sell in order to both meet demand and consistently maintain a given quality level. The more general big picture looks like Figure 1-4.

The Role of Distributors

Okay, so you have all the pieces in place to make a guitar, but your work is still not done. The finished guitar must be distributed to the consumer, the guitarist. There are several ways to do this. You can have the guitar shipped directly from your factory—probably your garage if you're just starting out—to the consumer (as in Figure 1-4). This is known as selling direct, but there are several problems with this. One problem has to do with service. If something on the guitar breaks during shipping, or the customer breaks the guitar within the warranty period, he or she has to ship it all the way back to your factory to get it fixed. Now this may not be a problem when both your business and your customer are in the same city, but if they are far away from each other, you have a problem. The turnaround time between shipping the guitar for service and receiving the fixed guitar is minimum one week, especially if you use ground freight. So, unless you can be sure you won't have any returns and your product is maintenance free, selling direct can be costly. Another problem with selling direct is that as a new guitar maker, you have to spend some time convincing guitarists to purchase your guitars instead of buying them from existing, more established guitar makers. Again, if your customers are in the same city as your business, then this may not be a problem. However, if your potential customers are miles away, then instead of spending your time making guitars, you have to spend it promoting your product.

The alternative to selling direct to customers is to use a distributor. For guitar makers, these distributors are commonly known as dealers. Salespeople at the

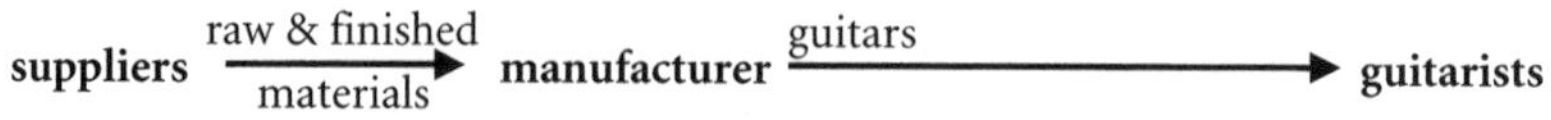

Figure 1-4. *The big picture: guitar maker as manufacturer*

dealership are responsible for promoting your guitars and providing customer service. Most dealers also have repair personnel that will fix and maintain your guitars. Typically, your guitars will only get sent back to you in extreme cases having to do with major product defects, such as a cracked guitar body. So, using a distributor allows you to focus on what you do best—building guitars—and the dealers can focus on what they do best—selling and servicing those guitars. Our big picture now looks like Figure 1-5.

Note that each of the participants (agents) in the "big picture" makes a contribution to the final product. The contribution can be material, as is the case with the suppliers and guitar maker, or service-based, such as the guitar repairs that the dealers provide. In short, each agent in the picture adds to the value contributed by the preceding agent. The big picture can thus be thought of as a *value chain*. Any business that makes a product has a value chain (see Figure 1-6), with material and service-based value flowing left to right and monetary value flowing back from right to left. The money flowing into the business from the upstream agents (distributors) denotes *revenues,* and money flowing out of the business to downstream agents (suppliers) denotes *costs.* A business's *profits* are its revenues minus costs (cash-based profits = revenues − costs).

One business's value chain can differ from another's in terms of the actual participants and number of participants in each category—that is, the number of suppliers/distributors. Moreover, a given agent can have several subcategories. A guitar maker's distributors, for example, could consist of wholesalers who buy the guitars in bulk quantities, such as 1,000 units of a given guitar. Buying guitars in bulk allows wholesalers to receive big discounts. The wholesaler then marks up the guitar prices and sells them to retailers (the guitar dealers).

Figure 1-5. *The big picture: where the distributors fit in*

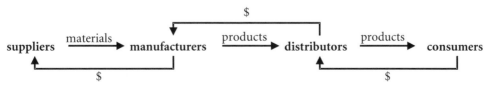

Figure 1-6. *The big picture: the generic value chain*

The Value Chain and the Web

The concept of a value chain is a useful tool for Web developers. It identifies at least four areas where the Web can be used to add value for a company. Remember that your goal is not to produce Web sites that are simply online brochures or online catalogs. Instead, your goal is to produce Web sites that add value to a company. To accomplish this, first note that all participants along the value chain contribute value to the product. Thus, by using the Web to help or enhance the activities of the participants, the Web itself adds value. There are four general areas where the Web can be used to add value to a company.

1. *Between the manufacturer and its suppliers.* A straightforward example would be suppliers like Georgia Bonded Fibers *(www.bontex.com),* who place product specification data sheets online for manufacturers. A more sophisticated example would be a Web-based auction where suppliers bid to supply parts at the lowest price to manufacturers.

2. *Within a company.* Companies like Silicon Graphics, Cadence, and Booz Allen Hamilton have set up Intranets for effectively sharing knowledge and speeding up information distribution among employees.

3. *Between a company and its distributors.* Lamson & Sessions Co., a $280 million electrical parts manufacturer in Beachwood, Ohio, uses electronic data interchange (EDI) to transmit and receive purchase orders, advance ship notices, order acknowledgments, and send invoices to customers like Wal-Mart and Ace Hardware. The Web can be used as a low-cost replacement for EDI.

4. *Between the distributor and the consumer.* By far this is the most common use of the Web. The Web is used as a means of advertising products and purchasing products; the examples are too numerous to mention. More innovative uses of the Web between consumers and distributors seek to aggregate consumers' buying power to negotiate lower prices for products or services.

In short, the value chain shows us that just using the Web to create electronic brochures and catalogs underutilizes its potential: The distributor mainly benefits from such a site. This can have a positive, albeit indirect, effect on the downstream participants, namely the suppliers and manufacturer. For example, an increase in dealer sales means increased revenues for the manufacturer and thus increased revenues for the suppliers. However, if a manufacturer asks for a Web site, an electronic catalog may not be the most direct means of adding value.

Instead, a Web site that improves the interaction between supplier and manufacturer, or between manufacturer and distributor, provides more direct benefits.

More generally, between agents in a value chain, the Web can be used to lower the cost of an interaction (item 1), improve the timing of an interaction (item 3), or provide a different way of performing an existing action (item 4: online advertising/purchasing). Within an agent, the Web can be used as a tool for more efficiently distributing knowledge and information within a given organization (item 2).

We've been focusing on the activities of a single business and how the Web can be used to support that business's activities. However, a business usually has to contend with other businesses, or competitors, for its products or services. Besides being a support tool, the Web can also be a strategic tool that helps a business compete more effectively. In the next chapter, we examine the role competition plays in shaping the activities of our fictitious business. We'll see that the big picture stays the same, but the firm will have to acquire additional departments such as research and development or marketing to stay competitive. We'll also discuss different ways a company can use the Web as a strategic tool.

CHAPTER 2

Competition and the Web

Executive Summary

Very few businesses are the sole maker or provider of a product or service. There are usually other businesses in the same field—the competition. This chapter examines the effects of competition on a business and covers general strategies for competing with other businesses. A better understanding of competition will help you identify more diverse ways of using the Web to help your client's or your own business compete more effectively.

Objectives

After reading this chapter you should be able to:

- *Define competition and describe the effects of competition on a business*

- *Outline general strategies (moves) for competing*

- *Describe some high-level ways the Web can be used to support strategic moves*

Introduction

A manufacturer is rarely the sole provider of a product. Typically there are other businesses producing something similar. These businesses are known as *competitors*. Even when a business is the first to enter a given field, it is highly likely that another business will emerge to produce a similar product, especially if sales are good. Thus, a business needs to set goals and plan out a strategy for implementing those goals, one that takes into account the existence of competitors. The aim of this chapter is to describe basic strategic moves that a business can make and how the Web can be used to support those moves.

Understanding the Effects of Competition:
The Case of the Guitar Maker

To understand competition and its effect on a company, let us imagine once again that you are a guitar maker. As you may recall from Chapter 1, your value chain looks like Figure 2-1.

We need to make some assumptions in order to see better the effects of competition on the guitar maker. Assume the materials used to build one guitar cost $250; this cost includes the wood, electronics, strings, and so on. Further assume that you make 1,000 guitars each year and that dealers purchase all your guitars. Before selling your guitars to the dealers, you mark up each one $750 to cover the costs of equipment used to make the guitars and to pay staff. Thus, the cost to the dealers is $1,000 per guitar (wholesale price). The dealer marks up the guitars 100 percent, charging $2,000 per guitar (retail or list price). The dealers mark up the guitars to cover activities like promoting your guitars, paying the guitar salespeople, and paying the technicians that service guitars. Finally, assume that guitarists buy 1,000 guitars every year from the dealers (guitarists love buying next year's model). The value chain with these numbers is in Figure 2-2.

Profits can be calculated by looking at cash flowing into the agents (revenues) and cash flowing out of the business (costs). The suppliers get $250,000 from you for buying their materials (your cost: 1,000 units × $250/unit).

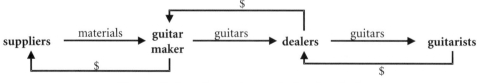

Figure 2-1. *Our guitar maker's value chain*

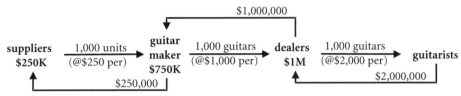

Figure 2-2. *Profits without competition*

For pedagogical reasons, we'll make the (unreasonable) assumption that the suppliers have zero costs, so the money you give them amounts to their profits. You get $1,000,000 of revenues from the dealers (dealers' costs: 1,000 guitars at $1,000/guitar), yielding a profit of $750,000 for your company. The dealers get $2,000,000 of revenues (guitarists' cost: 1,000 guitars sold × $2,000/guitar) from the guitarists, yielding $1,000,000 of profits. And the guitarists get the guitars and value in terms of satisfaction.

Assuming you have no competition, this value chain also represents the *value ecology,* the entire system of agents that propagate value in a given industry. However, suppose another person (guitar maker 2) decides to make guitars (guitars2). One would expect that this guitar maker would compete with you for the guitarists' (consumers') business. Note, however, that guitar maker 2 also needs to get supplies and sell guitars to dealers. Thus, guitar maker 2 is competing with you for suppliers and dealers as well. So, with another guitar maker, the situation looks like Figure 2-3.

Let us assume that guitar maker 2 (1) produces the same number of guitars as you do, (2) has the same materials requirements, (3) pays the same amount to suppliers, and (4) charges the same amount to the dealers. Further assume that

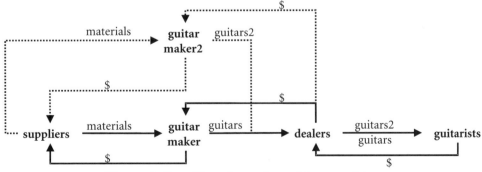

Figure 2-3. *The value ecology with competition*

the dealers charge you both the same price for your guitars and buy 1,000 guitars from each of you—2,000 guitars in all. The final important assumption we make is that demand remains constant—guitarists will only buy 1,000 guitars: 400 of your guitars and 600 of guitar maker 2's guitars. The value ecology looks like Figure 2-4.

What are the effects on the value ecology, specifically on profits? The big winner is the supplier, who makes $500K in profit, as opposed to $250K when you were the only guitar maker. Both guitar makers also win. You get the same level of profits as you did when you were the only guitar maker. Your consumers, the guitarists, also win; all 1,000 of them are happily playing new guitars. The big loser is the dealer. The dealer bought 2,000 guitars—1,000 from you and 1,000 from guitar maker 2. The dealers' costs were thus $2M (2,000 guitars @ $1,000/guitar). Unfortunately, only 1,000 guitarists bought these guitars, resulting in $2M in revenues, which in turn amounts to $0 in profits ($2M revenues − $2M costs).

The dealer now has 600 extra guitars from you (the dealer sold 400 of your guitars) and 400 extra guitars from your competitor (the dealer sold 600 guitar2s). What happens next is interesting. The dealer, being pessimistic, assumes that you will only sell 400 guitars next year. Likewise, the dealer assumes that guitar maker 2 will only sell 600 guitars next year. But remember, the dealer has 600 of your guitars sitting in storage and 400 guitars from your competitor. Thus, the dealer buys *zero* guitars from you and only 200 guitars from guitar maker 2 (see Figure 2-5).

What are the effects on the value ecology now? This time around, the suppliers still have the same level of profits ($500K). The dealers have $1.8M in profits. The guitarists are happy as well. However, both guitar makers lose this time. Guitar maker 2 suffers at least a $50K loss, and you suffer a $250K loss. Further-

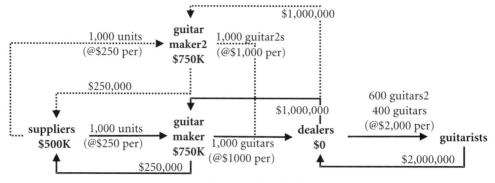

Figure 2-4. *Profits after first year*

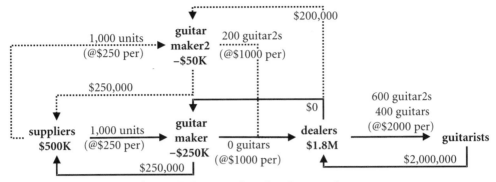

Figure 2-5. *Profits after the second year*

more, you have 1,000 extra guitars sitting in your warehouse, and guitar maker 2 has 800 extra guitars sitting in a warehouse. The dealers will only order 600 guitars from guitar maker 2 and 200 of your guitars (dealer still has 200 guitars left over from year one, and demand for your guitars is at 400/year). There are enough guitars in your warehouses, so this time neither you nor guitar maker 2 buys any supplies from the suppliers. Thus, the suppliers finally lose (see Figure 2-6).

The point is that everyone along the value chain is affected by the presence of competition. The consumer (guitarist) wins in each case, but the agents both upstream and downstream from the manufacturer can be negatively affected for a time. The addition of a competitor destroys equilibrium, and when information is slow in arriving, loss for all agents may occur until a new equilibrium is established. Now let's jump into the future and assume that the agents indeed

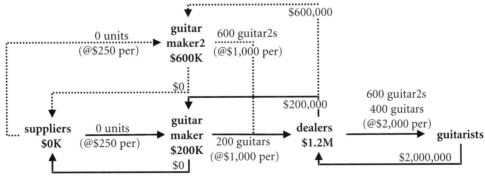

Figure 2-6. *Profits after the third year*

settle into an equilibrium. All things the same, at equilibrium the value ecology looks like Figure 2-7.

So, in the presence of competition, you as a guitar maker only get $300K in profits versus $750K when you were the only guitar maker around. The 60 percent loss in market share to guitar maker 2 results in a 60 percent decrease in profits! Clearly this is a bad thing. Everyone else along the value chain either benefits or settles at the same level of profits. So, for you a key question becomes What can I do to minimize the effects of competition on my company? This is a question of *strategy*.

Basic Strategic Moves

To minimize the effects of competition, companies have a variety of strategic moves at their disposal. In this section we examine some of the key moves suggested by the value ecology diagram and how the Web can support these moves.

Move 1: Locking In/Locking Out

One obvious move suggested by the value ecology diagrams is to *lock in business partners* and *lock out competitors*. In our guitar maker example, your business partners are your suppliers and your distributors. By locking in suppliers so that they provide supplies solely to you, competitors will not have the raw materials needed to build their products. Similarly, by locking in distributors so that they sell only your product, the consumers have no choice but to buy your product. A big problem with the lock in/lock out move is that both suppliers and distribu-

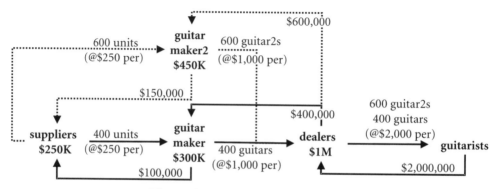

Figure 2-7.   *Profits at equilibrium*

tors may be unwilling to participate, particularly when the business requesting it is small. One way to use the Web to achieve a kind of "virtual" lock-in is to give suppliers and distributors limited access to a corporate Intranet (an Extranet). Our guitar maker, for example, could give distributors easy access to a Web-based ordering system. Such a system would make it easy to both see what items were in stock (for example, red guitars) and to order those items. By using the Web to make it easier for suppliers or distributors to order your products instead of a competitors', you increase the chances of them ordering from you. In effect, you achieve a kind of virtual lock-in with your business partners.

Move 2: Integrating (Buying Out) Business Partners

The second basic move is to *integrate business partners.* This is similar to the lock in/lock out strategy, but instead of negotiating fixed-length contracts so that suppliers and distributors exclusively provide for your company, you make key suppliers and distributors an actual *part* of your company by buying them out. Similar to the lock in/lock out strategy, this move is not a viable option for small businesses, as buying another business requires a lot of money. Besides providing information about business partners, it is not clear how the Web can be used to assist this move.

Move 3: Integrating (Buying Out) Competitors

Closely related to integrating business partner is *buying out competitors.* In our example of the guitar maker, you would buy out guitar maker 2. The benefits are clear: You recover any market share lost to competitors. Such a move, however, is typically available only to large businesses because of the great expense involved. Moreover, when there are many competitors, this option is typically not viable even for large businesses. Beyond providing information about competitors, it is difficult to see how the Web can directly be used to help with this move.

Move 4: Marketing

The fourth basic move is to understand why your competitors are outperforming you. There are four basic reasons why a competitor would outperform your company: (1) your company is selling the wrong product, (2) your company is selling the right product but at the wrong price, (3) consumers are unaware that your product exists or do not have enough information to decide to buy your product, or (4) consumers do not have an easy way to purchase your product—for example, there may be no dealer in their area. In short, your company needs to do a better job of *marketing* by following these steps:

1. Figure out which product to produce.

2. Price this product accordingly.

3. Promote the product to consumers.

4. Place the product in a location that consumers have easy access to.

These four activities are commonly referred to as "the four P's of marketing": product, price, promotion, and placement. Your company needs a marketing department to carry out these activities. The marketing department works closely with research and development (R&D)—marketing determines what the company should do (and how much to produce at what price), and R&D figures out how to do it.

You can use the Web to gather the marketing information needed for the four key marketing activities (see Figure 2-8), which is an important function since time lags in information were responsible for our sample company losing money in the short term. Note that the Web can be used to gather marketing information not only from your distributors but from your consumers as well.

Move 5: Reduce Business Costs

The fifth basic move is to reduce the costs of doing business. Given a certain level of demand for your product (in our example, 400 guitars), instead of increasing demand to increase profits, you reduce costs in order to increase profits. The value ecology diagrams show that there are several ways a business can reduce costs to increase profits.

First, and most obvious, is to lower the cost of supplies. If a business can negotiate lower prices for supplies (for example, through bulk discounts), it can realize a profit. A business can also find lower-cost suppliers to do business with.

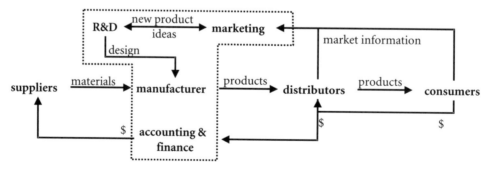

Figure 2-8. *Adding marketing and R&D to the value chain*

To see the benefits of reducing costs, assume you find a supplier that will provide the same guitar parts for a hundred dollars less ($150 versus $250). Instead of paying $100K for supplies, you now pay $60K; the $40K you save becomes profit ($340K instead of $300K).

A second less obvious approach is to reduce operating costs. Up to this point, we've assumed in our example that your profits were calculated as revenue from guitar sales to dealers minus the costs of supplies ($300K at equilibrium). Yet, there are also *internal costs* you must subtract, such as employee salaries. For example, you could have two employees, each making $50K, working at your guitar factory. In this case, your actual profits would be $200K. In short, by reducing the costs of doing business with your partners or reducing internal operating costs, you can realize higher profits and thus compete more effectively.

In closing, there are many moves you can take to make your business more competitive or to reduce the effects of competition on your business—and we've just scratched the surface in this chapter. Collectively these moves constitute your business's strategy. This chapter's aim was to get you thinking about ways of using the Web as a strategic instrument and not merely as a support tool. Of course, the question of how exactly one goes about discovering these strategic and support uses of the Web still remains. Part of the answer lies in the realization that all strategic moves and business activities rely on information storage, retrieval, transformation, and propagation. The other part of the answer relies on a technique—Web Business Engineering—which allows one to analyze this information activity and design Web-based solutions around it.

Next we'll address the first part of the answer. So far, we've primarily focused on the movement of physical goods along the value chain. However, information plays a critical role in supporting the movement of physical goods. In the next chapter, we examine the important role information plays in the value chain and the different high-level ways the Web can be used to assist such information activities.

CHAPTER THREE

The Role of Information in the Value Chain

Executive Summary

We have seen that the value chain is a set of agents transforming and moving *physical* goods. However, *information* plays a critical role in supporting the movement of those physical goods. In this chapter we examine how information supports the physical value chain and how one can, in turn, use the Web to support this information. Physical goods differ in terms of how much knowledge users need to effectively manipulate them. For such products the Web can play more than a supporting role; it becomes an important instructional tool. Finally, we look at how the Web can completely transform the value chain for pure-information products and end with a discussion of how the Web enables different business models. With the completion of these first three chapters, you should have a much broader sense of where you can use the Web.

Objectives

After reading this chapter you should be able to:

■ *Describe how information supports the value chain*

■ *Distinguish between knowledge-intensive and pure-information products*

■ *Identify ways of using the Web to support knowledge-intensive and pure-information products*

■ *Explain the autonomous Web business model*

Introduction

In Chapters 1 and 2, we saw that the value chain is a collection of agents that transforms physical goods, starting with supplies and ending with actual products in the consumer's hands. Not depicted, however, was the important role of information in supporting the transformation and movement of goods. The Web is a perfect tool for supporting the information used in the value chain. But the Web can play far more than a supporting role, depending on the kind of product. Specifically, certain goods are *knowledge-intensive,* requiring a significant amount of knowledge to manipulate them effectively. Guitars are a perfect example of such a product, as are consumer electronics like VCRs. For such knowledge-intensive products, the Web can be an important channel for distributing the knowledge consumers need to use the products effectively. Finally, certain goods are composed primarily of information such as software and music. For these *pure-information* products, the Web can radically transform or even substitute for a business's entire value chain.

In short, businesses produce a continuum of products ranging from purely physical goods at one end to knowledge-intensive goods to pure-information products at the other end of the spectrum. One can use the Web to support each type of product in a different and useful way. In this chapter we examine the different ways that information supports the value chains for each of these products and how the Web can support this information. The chapter also presents a description of how the Web is creating entirely new models for doing business and describes one of them: the autonomous Web business.

How Information Supports the Value Chain for Physical Products

The value chains we've seen to this point depicted the exchange of material goods and money among suppliers, producers, distributors, and consumers. Yet there are also complex information interchanges between these agents, supporting the exchange of these material goods. Take the dealer and the guitarist. Prior to purchasing a guitar, a guitarist typically talks with a salesperson at the dealership about which guitar to purchase. The dealership in turn provides important services for the guitarist, such as fixing and maintaining guitars (see Figure 3-1).

You can use the Web to replace many of the information interactions between the guitarist and the dealer (see Figure 3-2). The dealer can put his inventory online to allow online purchases. In addition, service-related information and basic maintenance information—such as tuning, setting a guitar's intonation, and adjusting the guitar's truss rod—can also be placed online. When customers perform basic maintenance themselves, the dealers have more opportunity to perform higher-value-added activities, such as guitar repair.

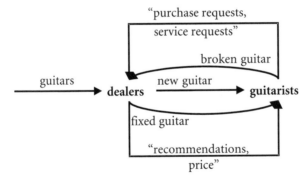

Figure 3-1. *The information a guitarist gets at a dealership*

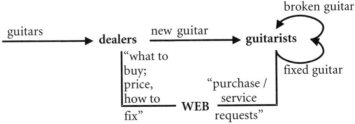

Figure 3-2. *Using the Web for guitar-related information*

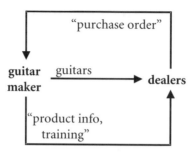

Figure 3-3.   *Information exchanged between a guitar maker and dealers*

Between dealer and guitar maker, the key information exchanged is purchase orders. However, the guitar maker also gives the dealers new product literature and provides training for new products (see Figure 3-3).

All this information exchanged verbally or on paper can also be placed online. Because product information is typically on paper, it is very easy to transform it into a Web page. Moreover, the various Web multimedia vehicles make it very easy to transform training information into (for example) streaming video (see Figure 3-4).

Finally, the information exchanged between the guitar maker and the suppliers includes shipping information and inventory information (not shown). In general, there is a complex information infrastructure underlying the movement of physical goods along the value chain. Thus, when deciding on a Web strategy, there are actually two value chains that we should consider: the value chain of physical goods and the information value chain that supports the movement of physical goods (see Figure 3-5).

One obvious way of using the Web to add value is by having it mediate the storage and distribution of the information (see Figure 3-6). By streamlining the information propagation, the Web adds value to all agents in the chain by, among others, reducing the cost of information transactions, improving the timing and

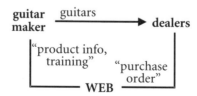

Figure 3-4.   *Using the Web to mediate guitar maker/dealer information*

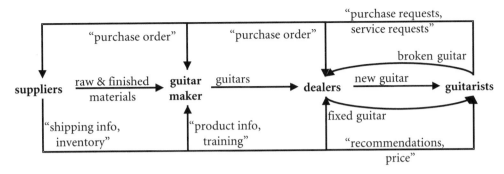

Figure 3-5. *Physical and informational value chains*

quality of the information exchanged, and increasing the quantity of information that can be exchanged.

Used in this manner the Web plays an important, albeit supporting, role in the physical value chain. For purely physical goods, this is the primary way one uses the Web to add value to the intermediate agents in the chain. The consumer gets some benefits as well, but they are largely indirect. This is not to say that the Web can only play a supporting role. In the following section we examine products where information is an important component of the product itself and where the Web, consequentially, can play more of a prominent role in adding value directly to the consumer.

Knowledge-Intensive Products

To use certain kinds of products effectively, consumers need a fair amount of knowledge about them. Consumer electronics like VCRs and camcorders are good examples of such products. For these *knowledge-intensive products*, information is just as important as the physical good itself. The Web, being a flexible information technology, can be molded to better provide this knowledge to users.

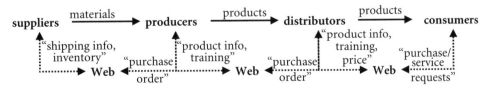

Figure 3-6. *The Web as a key component of an informational value chain*

And it's not just high-tech products that are knowledge intensive. As it turns out, our example product, the guitar, is a knowledge-intensive product as well. Let's take a closer look at knowledge-intensive products, once again using the guitar as our example.

A guitar is a product that consumers can't just buy and start using. The typical guitar player possesses a lot of knowledge about how to play and maintain guitars. In addition to playing and maintaining guitars, guitarists have in-depth knowledge about how to *combine* the guitar with other complementary products, like amplifiers and effects pedals, in order to either reproduce the tones of famous guitarists (e.g., Jimi Hendrix) or simply to produce good tones. The guitarist's knowledge can be placed into three knowledge categories (see Figure 3-7): how to play (operational knowledge), how to maintain a guitar (maintenance knowledge), and how to combine the guitar with other guitar-related products (combinatorial knowledge). Operational, maintenance, and combinatorial knowledge apply to almost all products, not just guitars. What differs among products is the amount of knowledge the consumer must acquire in the three categories before he or she can use the product.

Clearly, not having such knowledge limits the number of consumers that will purchase guitars or other knowledge-intensive products. To get around this, manufacturers have to design usability into products and/or include huge instruction manuals, both of which contribute to a more expensive final product. Today, however, with almost everyone connected to the Web, much of the paper-based instructional material can be placed online. And although usability is always an important product feature, there are certain products like guitars where you can't build in usability—in other words, you can't build into the guitar the knowledge needed to play it. Once again, one can use the multimedia, interactive features of the Web to assist consumers in learning the necessary information needed to use a product effectively.

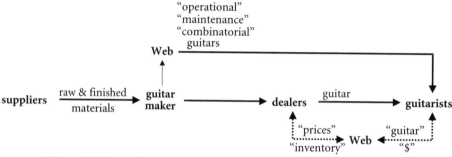

Figure 3-7. *Three categories of knowledge associated with guitars*

Using the Web as a knowledge provider can have strategic advantages as well. Imagine you—as a guitar maker—do your marketing and discover that a lot of people want to play guitar but they don't want to hassle with finding a good teacher and going to lessons on a regular basis. So what you do in response is put *free* instructional material on the Web, with the caveat that only the users that buy your guitars can access this material. You've essentially captured a niche through clever use of technology! There are many different ways of using the Web to support knowledge-intensive products, and this example is just one possibility. All products have some knowledge dimension that you can use the Web to exploit. Web Business Engineering can help you find some of these possibilities.

Pure Information-Based Products

There is a special class of producers that create products that are primarily information based. These producers include businesses in the software and music industries. Their products have relied on a traditional value chain for their distribution. For example, the value chain for software looks much the same as that of any other manufacturer of a physical good (see Figure 3-8).

However, the emergence of the Web radically changes the value chain for software and other information-based products. The Web, for example, can substitute for the entire distribution side of the value chain. Specifically, instead of distributing software through dealers, software makers can distribute it via the Web. In fact, many software companies are allowing consumers to directly purchase their programs from their Web sites. Thus, the Web becomes more than just a supporting technology or a knowledge provider; it is an integral component of a company's value chain (see Figure 3-9).

How is it possible that software can bypass the normal distribution channels? Unlike products like guitars that are largely physical and whose distributors

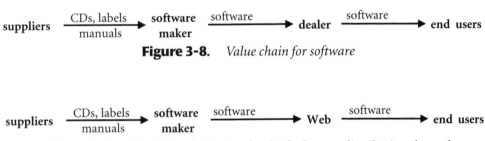

Figure 3-8.   *Value chain for software*

Figure 3-9.   *The Web substituting for the dealer as a distribution channel*

provide important training and maintenance services, the typical software dealer neither trains nor maintains the software. If there is training, it is usually providing by some outside agency that specializes in teaching end users specific packages—for example, certified training programs for Microsoft Excel. Also, software dealers don't perform software maintenance. If software breaks, it is most likely due to an error in the program, and "maintenance" in these situations amounts to the dealer exchanging the software for a newer version (if it exists). As such, the primary value-added from the software dealer is convenience. So, if the Web can provide the same or better level of convenience, it can substitute as a distribution channel, and it does. Indeed, software companies already allow software updates to be downloaded from the Web, often with a simple click of a button (see Figure 3-10). Currently, Web-based software training is not very sophisticated, with frequently asked question (FAQ) Web pages representing a basic form of training. However, as companies become more sophisticated using the various multimedia Web vehicles, we can expect interactive, video streaming to be a common form of Web-based training.

Finally, the Web can also eliminate the supplies used to package the software. These supplies are an artifact of software makers using the traditional, physical value chain. With the Web distributing the software directly into the consumer's computer, CDs and labels are no longer necessary. Moreover, the software manuals can be eliminated and their content placed online instead. So we end up with a total reconfiguration of the software maker's value chain (see Figure 3-11).

Figure 3-10.   *The Web as more than a distribution channel*

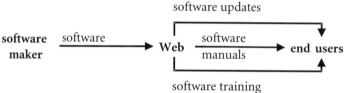

Figure 3-11.   *The Web replacing the supply side of the value chain*

Information goods are also changing the rules for products. In the past, a physical good would never be released until it was completed and the product met a certain quality standard. To release a defective product was unthinkable because, among other reasons, it was prohibitively expensive to retool manufacturing to fix design flaws, to recall products, and to distribute and install replacements. However, information products have alleviated these costs. Take software. If a defect occurs in a released piece of software, the software maker can simply place a "fix" on its Web site. The fix consists of a new version of the software along with an install program that will automatically replace the old version of the software with the new one. The user simply downloads the fix and runs the install program. This process can be automated even further. If the user is logged on, the software can automatically check if there are fixes available and install them, all in the background without the user's intervention. Thus, many companies not only release early software prototypes with known bugs, they also charge consumers money for them!

In closing, I want to emphasize again that my goal is not to provide comprehensive coverage of all the different ways the Web can be used to support information products and the information side of the value chain. Rather my intent is to get you, as a Web entrepreneur or Web consultant, to start thinking about broader ways of using the Web. And the Web Business Engineering techniques taught in the next section will show you how to discover more specific uses.

Now as a bonus, let's end this chapter with an examination of a new kind of business model made possible by the Web. In this business model, not only is the product pure information, but the business itself and the entire value chain is information based. Except for the consumer, no other humans or equipment (besides a computer) are involved.

New Business Models: The Autonomous Business

A common saying is that businesses need to build community around their Web sites. Unfortunately, what most businesses think of as a Web community is a chat room on their Web site that large numbers of users regularly visit. However, it's not clear how this notion of community adds value to their businesses. One obvious way that businesses can exploit their user community is by selling advertisers space on their Web site for placing various kinds of ads (see Figure 3-12). Thus, businesses (producers in the diagram) can make money from advertising in addition to whatever product they're selling on their Web site.

Figure 3-12. *Using a Web community to generate revenues through advertising*

We can take this basic model and transform it into an entirely new way of doing business online. Under this new business model you, as a Web entrepreneur, set up what looks like the Web site in Figure 3-12 with an important difference: This Web site starts off with *minimal* content and sells nothing. Specifically, instead of creating a content-intensive Web site that sells a product or provides some service, you create just enough content to attract consumers. I refer to such content as *bootstrap content.* Now, in addition to this bootstrap content, you place interactive mechanisms—such as forms—that allow consumers to contribute their own content (see Figure 3-13).

The role of you as a producer becomes negligible at this point! Quite recursively, the consumers of the information become both suppliers and producers of it (see Figure 3-14).

If the content of your Web site is organized around a community topic, your site should attract other users as well. Over time, the number of consumers grows to the point where you can sell advertising to generate revenues. Then you take an active role again, signing up advertisers and selling advertising space on your site. With the advertisers set up, you once again remove yourself from the process and simply collect revenues from the advertisers. The revenues are based on a number of advertiser payment models that include pay-per-click, pay-per-impression,

producers $\xrightarrow[\text{mechanism}]{\text{content}}$ **Web commune**

Figure 3-13. *Content mechanisms for generating community*

Figure 3-14. *Consumers as producers*

pay-per-lead, and percentage-of-sales, to name a few. This situation is depicted graphically in Figure 3-15.

This is an ingenious business model for many reasons. Besides creating the bootstrap content, which is minimal, and the content collection forms, you do very little work adding new content. Your users do all the work for you. They add all the content, they attract other users, and they provide the "eyeballs" that you sell to the advertisers. In short, the community generates itself, the content, and your revenues! (For examples of two such Web sites I created that implement this model, see *www.datingexpert.com* and *www.yesnomaybe.com.* Another good example of such a site is *www.harmony-central.com.*) Some details in this model have been omitted, especially how the community generates more community. Most of these issues will be addressed later in the book, specifically in Chapter 14 on memetic marketing.

At this point, you should have a broader sense of how and where to use the Web than you did before. You should also have a lot of questions about how to identify more specific ways of using the Web to add value to a business. These questions will be answered in later chapters. However, first you must understand one last business idea: the concept of value and how to value a Web site.

Figure 3-15. *Using advertising for generating revenues*

CHAPTER FOUR

Value and Valuing a Web Site

Executive Summary

As a Web consultant an important part of your job is convincing business managers to adopt your Web proposals, and as a Web entrepreneur you often need to decide which of several Web businesses to start. Both activities require knowing how to value a Web site. In this chapter we'll cover several techniques for valuing Web sites and technology projects in general, the most important of which are return on investment (ROI) and net present value (NPV).

Objectives

After reading this chapter you should be able to:

- *Calculate and know the intuitions behind return on investment (ROI)*

- *Calculate and know the intuitions behind net present value (NPV)*

- *Explain Payback and IRR*

Introduction

Up to this point we've used the term *value* qualitatively. A Web site was said to have high value if it significantly increased a business's revenues or reduced its costs, and if a Web *site* accomplished either of these results, it qualified as a *Web business.* However, what exactly does it mean to "significantly" increase revenues and reduce costs? Moreover, given two Web sites that both propose to significantly increase revenues and reduce costs, which one is better? These are some of the questions you will encounter either as a consultant trying to sell your Web site proposal to a potential client or as an entrepreneur trying to decide what type of online business to start. The answers to such questions require a more quantitative definition of value.

Unfortunately, many Web consultants and entrepreneurs place too much emphasis on getting a Web site's technical details right and not enough time quantifying its value. Naive consultants believe a technically good solution will sell itself, and naive entrepreneurs believe a technically flashy site will attract and retain users. Now for a small population of potential clients or users this is probably true. But ultimately, the quality of a site is determined by how much value it adds to the potential client's business or to the user. A business-savvy manager will look beyond a proposed Web site's flashy technical details and instead try to determine what value it adds to his or her business. A smart user will eventually stop going to a site if it doesn't provide high enough value. So the more adept you are at determining this value, the more likely you are to succeed in selling your site proposal (consultant) or building a site that attracts and retains customers (entrepreneur). Both activities require some way of quantifying the value of a site.

We'll examine several standard ways of measuring value that businesses have adopted. The first metric is return on investment (ROI). However, the simplest form of ROI does not take into account the time value of money—a dollar today is not the same as a dollar tomorrow—so we will examine another metric known as net present value (NPV) and briefly touch on internal rate of return (IRR).

The Web Site Proposal

To simplify our treatment of the concept of value, the following examples assume you are a Web consultant trying to sell a Web site proposal to a potential client who has several proposals—only one of which is yours—to choose from. However, the material is still relevant for Web entrepreneurs. Just put yourself in the role of the client and pretend that each proposal is a different kind of business that you are thinking of starting up and that you have to pick one of them. A final, less obvious simplification is that all numerical values are about an order of magnitude smaller than they ought to be. I did this intentionally, as I believe people learn better when presented with magnitudes with which they are familiar. Now let's take a look at what a business manager does.

The role of a business manager can be likened to that of a computer programmer, but instead of assembling symbols into working programs that run on a computer, the business manager assembles resources (people and technology) into processes that "run" in a business. The preference, when designing new processes, is to use existing, in-house resources. However, there are cases where the solution calls for expertise or technology that cannot be easily found or developed in-house. In these cases, the manager must rely on outside consultants or other service providers to deliver the solution. The process of deciding on an outside solution can be complex. There are many companies that can provide a solution (solution providers), but they may differ along a number of dimensions such as quality, price, delivery time, and features.

Managers typically obey the following procedure when looking for an outside service. The manager first mails out a request for information (RFI) document to potential solution providers. This is a document asking the potential solution providers for general information about the products and services that their company provides. Next, the manager reviews the responses with his or her management team. The team narrows down a list of good solution providers. These solution providers are then sent a request for proposal (RFP) document that outlines the specific solution the manager is looking for, along with requests for important information such as price, delivery schedule, and maintenance plans. The solution providers then send in their proposals, and the manager must select the best proposal.

This is the typical proposal scenario. It should be noted, however, that mature businesses know who the best consultants are, so to save time, they often combine the RFI with the RFP. Given a set of proposals, the key question becomes How does a manager select the best proposal? Intuitively, the best proposal is the most valuable one. Let's turn our intuition into something more tangible and quantitative.

Value: Return on Investment (ROI)

Instead of thinking like a Web consultant, put yourself in the role of a manager who is evaluating a Web proposal. Assume you are a manager for a guitar manufacturer and you have received three proposals for creating your Web site. Proposal A describes the features of your Web site and the cost. Proposal B describes the features of the Web site, the cost of the Web site, and also your economic gain from sales and advertisers (revenues). Proposal C is similar to proposal B but promises more revenues; C also costs more than B. Finally, assume that you have $10,000 in your budget for investing in new proposals. A summary of these proposals is shown in Figure 4-1. Which proposal does the manager go with?

Note that you have a $10,000 budget, so you definitely can afford all three proposals. However, a good manager will immediately rule out Proposal A because Proposal A's profits cannot be determined without knowledge of A's revenues. Both Proposals B and C contain revenue and cost information, so their values can be determined. It does not matter that Proposal A costs less than B or C. Without a knowledge of A's revenues, a good manager will reject Proposal A outright. This leaves you with two proposals, B and C, but it is not readily apparent which proposal is better. For instance, Proposal C makes more money than B ($6,000 versus $5,000), but it costs more as well ($5,000 versus $4,000). Both proposals make about the same profit (revenue − cost, B: $5,000 − $4,000 = $1,000; C: $6,000 − $5,000 = $1,000). Which proposal is better?

Using Intuition to Determine Which Proposal Is Better

Intuitively Proposal B is better than C simply because you can make the same amount of money ($1,000) for less cost ($4,000 for B versus $5,000 for C). Furthermore, if you go with Proposal B, you have more money left over ($5,000 for B versus $4,000 for C). You can put this money in the bank, for example, so that at the end of the year you get money from both Proposal B and from the bank or other investments. In general, given two projects with the same profits

Proposal	Revenue	Cost	Profit
A	Not specified	$2,000	Unknown
B	$5,000	$4,000	$1,000
C	$6,000	$5,000	$1,000

Figure 4-1. *Profits for Proposals A, B, and C*

but with different costs, the good manager always selects the project that has the lower cost. This leaves extra money around for investing in other projects. Problems occur when you have two proposals with similar, but not exact, profits and costs.

Look at Figure 4-2. Is the lower profit that you make with Proposal X ($400) at a lower cost ($600) better than the higher profits you make with Proposal Y ($500) at a higher cost ($1,000)? You could always go with the proposal that makes the higher profits (Proposal Y because it has higher profits than Proposal X). But is more always better?

Proposal	Revenue	Cost	Profit
X	$1,000	$600	$400
Y	$1,000	$1,000	$500

Figure 4-2.   *Profits for Proposals X and Y*

Let's return to Proposals B and C. Suppose Proposal B costs $1 more, which reduces profits by $1 (see Figure 4-3). Now Proposal C makes slightly more profit than Proposal B ($1,000 for C versus $999 for B).

Proposal	Revenue	Cost	Profit
B	$5,000	$4,001	$999
C	$6,000	$5,000	$1,000

Figure 4-3.   *Modified Proposal B. Proposal B costs $1 more*

Intuitively, Proposal B is still better than Proposal C because the profits are about the same, and B costs way less than C. And here we come to the crux of the problem: How far apart do the profits have to be before they are no longer "about the same?" How far apart do the costs have to be before one proposal is no longer "way less" than the other? Intuitions are nice for getting quick estimates of a proposal's worth, and when the numbers are just right, intuitions are sufficient. It's for those proposals like B and C where the numbers are "close" that it would be nice to have some kind of objective measure to rely on. Such a measure would not only agree with our intuitions when profits are close and costs are spread out but would help us determine which proposal is better when the numbers are not so obvious. The most common such measure is known as *return on investment (ROI)*.

Using Return on Investment (ROI) to Determine Proposal Value

ROI in its simplest form is defined as profits divided by costs (see Figure 4-4). ROI is also known as a *profitability index*, and the proposal with the higher ROI is typically the better proposal. Let's first check if ROI agrees with our intuitions that Proposal B is better than C. The ROI for Proposal B is $1,000 / $4,000 = 1/4 = 0.25. The ROI for Proposal C is $1,000 / $5,000 = 1/5 = 0.20. ROI is usually expressed in terms of percentages (multiply by 100 and add the percent sign to the end), so the ROIs for Projects B and C are 25% and 20%, respectively (see Figure 4-5).

$$\text{ROI} = \text{Profits} / \text{Costs} = (\text{Revenues} - \text{Costs}) / \text{Costs}$$

Figure 4-4.   *Formula for return on investment (ROI)*

Proposal	Revenue	Cost	Profit	ROI
B	$5,000	$4,000	$1,000	0.25 = 25%
C	$6,000	$5,000	$1,000	0.20 = 20%

Figure 4-5.   *ROI for Proposals B and C*

Proposal B's ROI is higher than C's, thereby agreeing with our intuitions that B is better than C. What about the modified Proposal B (costs $1 more)? Does ROI still agree with our intuitions? The $1 increase in the cost of Proposal B results in an ROI of 24.9%, which is still higher than C, so Proposal B is still better (see Figure 4-6).

Proposal	Revenue	Cost	Profit	ROI
B'	$5,000	$4,001	$999	0.249 = 24.9%
C'	$6,000	$5,000	$1,000	0.20 = 20%

Figure 4-6.   *ROI for modified Proposal B, which costs $1 more*

Proposal	Revenue	Cost	Profit	ROI
X	$1,000	$600	$400	0.67 = 67%
Y	$1,500	$1,000	$500	0.50 = 50%

Figure 4-7.   *ROI for Proposals X and Y*

Thus, ROI agrees with our intuitions about which of Proposals B and C is better. We can now apply ROI to proposals X and Y to determine which one is better. ROI shows that despite X having less profit than Y ($400 versus $500), X has a higher ROI (67% versus 50%). Thus, X is the better proposal (see Figure 4-7).

To summarize, if you are a manager and are given the choice of several proposals, each with different revenues and costs, you generally go with the proposal that has the highest ROI. I say "generally" because the ROI has to be over a certain level as well. This level is typically 20%, or more than the manager can make investing his or her money in the bank or in other "safe" investments like mutual funds.

Net Present Value (NPV)

There's one glaring problem with the ROI, presented above as a measure of value: It ignores the time value of money; a dollar promised tomorrow is not the same as a dollar provided today. The time value of money is particularly relevant when one is dealing with Web sites because it typically takes a while for a Web site to start making money and even longer before the site is in steady state, bringing in a reliable stream of revenues. Let's assume you're a manager again and that you're given a proposal for a site that makes no money the year it begins operation, $1,000 the first full year of operation, $2,000 the second, and $3,000 the third. In business terms, you have *cash flows* of $1,000, $2,000, and $3,000 for years 1, 2, and 3, respectively. Assume that after the third year, the Web site is in steady state, bringing in roughly the same amount each year (see Figure 4-8).

Now suppose that the cost for this site is $5,000, similar to Proposal C (see Figures 4-1, 4-3, and 4-5), which had an ROI of 20%. What is your proposal's

Proposal	Year 0	Year 1	Year 2	Year 3
D	$0	$1,000	$2,000	$3,000

Figure 4-8.   *Revenue schedule for your proposed Web site*

ROI? The naive approach is to calculate revenues by simply adding up the money your site makes over those three years: $6,000 ($0 + $1,000 + $2,000 + $3,000). The site's cost is $5,000, so plugging revenue and cost into the ROI equation (see Figure 4-4) yields an ROI of 20%.

The problem is that Proposal D's ROI is exactly the same as Proposal C's, which doesn't seem right because Proposal C immediately makes $6,000, whereas it takes Proposal D over three years to make $6,000. You're also probably thinking that, through shrewd investing, you could take the $6,000 you make immediately from Proposal C and turn that into a lot more money than $6,000 in three years. So intuitively, Proposal C has more value than Proposal D, yet our treatment of ROI as presented in Figure 4-4 doesn't agree with our intuitions. Somehow we have to incorporate the fact that a dollar provided today is worth more than a dollar promised tomorrow.

The Time Value of Money After One Year

In proposals where money is distributed over several years, somehow we have to reduce the value, or *discount,* the money promised tomorrow. Once we do this, we can then add up the results and plug this discounted revenue into our ROI equation and get a better sense of the proposal's true value. But how do we discount the money promised tomorrow?

Let's use some actual numbers: Take the $1,000 that Proposal D promises a year from now (see Figure 4-8), and let's figure out how much it's worth to us today. Remember that intuitively $1,000 given to us a year from now is not worth as much as $1,000 given to us today because we could take today's $1,000 and invest it where we'll receive, say, 10% interest. After a year, the $1,000 given to us today will be worth more money than the $1,000 promised tomorrow—$1,100 to be exact (see Figure 4-9). We calculate the balance (B) after one year by taking our initial amount, $1,000 (also known as principal, P) and multiplying it by the interest rate of 10% (r), which yields $100, and then adding the $100 back to the principal. The equation for balance (B) given a principal amount (P) and an

Principal (P)	Rate (r)	Interest (after 1 year)	Balance (B) (after 1 year)
$1,000	10%	$100	$1,100

Figure 4-9.   *$1,000 in the bank after one year*

interest rate (r) after one year is seen in Figure 4-10. Using our figures, B = $1,000 × (1 + 0.10) = $1,000 + ($1,000 × 0.10) = $1,000 + $100 = $1,100.

$$B = P \times (1 + r)$$

Figure 4-10.   *Equation for balance after a year in the bank*

So we know that given an amount today we can figure out how much that amount is worth tomorrow (well, actually a year from now), given our formula for balance. Therefore, balance (B) in our equation is actually the future value of an amount today (P). Let's call that balance F (for future value) instead of B. Our equation becomes as seen in Figure 4-11.

$$F = P \times (1 + r)$$

Figure 4-11.   *General equation for future value* (F) *of a present value* (P) *after one year, given an interest rate* (r)

So, if we want to know how much something tomorrow (F) is worth in terms of something today (P), we work backwards from the future value equation. Let's return to Proposal D. Proposal D promises $1,000 a year from now. That $1,000 is a future amount (F). We want to know how much that amount is worth today. So we simply plug this value into our future value equation, resulting in $1,000 = P × (1 + r)$. What do we use as r? Let's use the interest rate of 10%. Our equation becomes $1,000 = P × (1 + .10)$ or $1,000 = P × 1.10$. Solving for P yields $P = $1,000/1.10 = $909.09. Thus, in terms of today's dollars (P), $1,000 tomorrow only equals $909.09 today.

Intuition Check

If this doesn't make sense yet, think of the result as saying that it takes an investment of $909.09 in the bank today to make $1,000 tomorrow. So if someone promises you $1,000 tomorrow (a year from now in Proposal D), it's the same thing as someone promising you $909.09 today. Or you can look at it this way: Suppose someone tells you, "I can give you $909.09 today or $975.00 dollars one year from now." Which would you take? You should take the $909.09 today because you can invest that in the bank, and one year from now, you'll have $1,000, which is more than the $975.00 that person would give you one year from now.

So, our situation stands as in Figure 4-12. Our final task is to come up with a general formula that determines the true (today's or the present) value of money that is promised more than one year from now.

Proposal	Year 0	Year 1	Year 2	Year 3
D	$0	$1,000 [$909.09]	$2,000	$3,000

Figure 4-12.   *Proposal D with first-year revenues discounted* [in brackets]

The Time Value of Money, in General

Determining the value of money promised more than a year from now is almost as simple as determining the present value for first-year revenues. Let's return to our 10% interest example. Suppose we invest $1,000 today. We know that one year from now, that $1,000 will turn into $1,100, which in turn will become $1,210 another year later: $1,210 = $1,100 × 1.10 = ($1,000 × 1.10) × 1.10. Yet another year later that $1,210 will turn into $1,331: $1,331 = $1,210 × 1.10 = (($1,000 × 1.10) × 1.10) × 1.10. And still another year later the $1,331 will turn into: $1,464.10 = $1,331 × 1.10 = ((($1,000 × 1.10) × 1.10) × 1.10) × 1.10. So, after four years, your $1,000 investment becomes $1,464.10. The pattern suggests the formula in Figure 4-13.

$$B = P \times (1 + r)^n$$

Figure 4-13.   *Bank equation balance after* n *years*

Where B is the ending balance after n years, given an initial deposit, or principal, of P and an interest rate of r. Once again, we can look at balance (B) as the future value (F) of our principal value (P). Then we can rewrite the equation as in Figure 4-14.

$$F = P \times (1 + r)^n$$
or
$$P = F/(1 + r)^n$$

Figure 4-14.   *The general equation for present value of a future cash flow*

Therefore, $1,000 is worth $1,464.10 four years from now, or $1,464.10 promised four years from now is only worth $1,000 today. We can use this equation to determine the true or present value of Proposal D's cash flows in terms of today's dollars. Take the $2,000 Proposal D expects in year 2. $2,000 = P × (1 + 0.10)^2, or P = $2,000/1.10^2 = $2,000 / (1.10 × 1.1) = $1,652.89. Similarly, in today's

Proposal	Year 0	Year 1	Year 2	Year 3
D	$0	$1,000 *[$909.09]*	$2,000 *[1,652.89]*	$3,000 *[$2,253.94]*

Figure 4-15. *Proposal D's discounted revenues (discounted cash flows). The discounted values are in brackets*

dollars, the $3,000 Proposal D expects in year 3 is worth: $P = \$3{,}000/1.10^{\wedge 3} = \$3{,}000/(1.10 \times 1.10 \times 1.10) = \$2{,}253.94$. Proposal D's discounted cash flows look like Figure 4-15.

Altogether, the total revenues that Proposal D promises are: $909.09 + $1,652.89 + $2,253.94 = $4,815.92. This total, also known as Proposal D's *net present value* (NPV), is much less than the $6,000 you get by simply adding together the undiscounted cash flows ($1,000 + $2,000 + $3,000). The general equation for NPV is in Figure 4-16.

$$\sum \frac{P_t}{(1 + r)^t}$$

Figure 4-16. *The general equation for net present value (NPV), where P_t is the cash flow at year t; r is the interest rate*

An important caveat: The cost of the project (in our example $5,000) is usually entered as a negative number for $t = 0$. So for year 0, $P0 = -\$5{,}000$. We can now update the equation for ROI to reflect NPV instead of total revenues (see Figure 4-17).

ROI = Profits / Costs = (NPV) / Costs

Figure 4-17. *Formula for return on investment (ROI)*

We can now determine the true ROI of Proposal D over four years, which amounts to: $(-\$5{,}000 + \$4{,}815.92)/\$5{,}000 = -4\%$. Surprisingly, Proposal D loses money! There is no way any rational manager would choose to fund D. This is a far cry from the 20% ROI that Proposal D supposedly makes when you don't discount cash flows. Thus, when the time value of money is taken into account, Proposal D is a very bad proposal, and the astute manager will always take the time value of money into account when determining a proposal's value.

Interest Rates, Discount Rates, and Risk Factors (r)

Throughout our discussion of NPV, we've used the 10% interest rate to discount Proposal D's cash flows. This 10% is also known as the discount rate, or risk factor, and in practice it is not simply an arbitrary interest rate. Managers use different discount rates depending on how risky the project is. The exact formulas for calculating discount rates are beyond the scope of this book. The interested reader can look up the capital asset pricing model (CAPM) for one such formula. The key idea is that speculative projects are discounted more heavily than safe projects that employ known technology. So, for example, the discount rate on a Web site that used a number of different, relatively unproven technologies like Java and databases might be 30% as opposed to 10% for a Web site that just used HTML. Depending on the discount rate used, your project may or may not make a client's ROI cutoff rate.

Finally, note that our calculations assumed that risk was not a problem with the future cash flows, which is usually not the case. There are a number of factors that may reduce expected cash flows, such as loss of market share or an increase in the cost of goods sold. Time is one of the greatest risks for an investment; generally, the longer the recovery or payback period, the greater the risk. When analyzing a proposal, managers not only do a present value analysis but may also assign probabilities to various cash flow scenarios to ultimately arrive at a risk-adjusted rate of return. This enables businesses to compare rates of return on an "apples to apples" basis.

Some Alternatives to NPV and ROI: Payback and IRR

NPV combined with ROI is the most common technique managers use to determine the value of a project, but two other techniques deserve mention if only because they are common enough that you will encounter them as a Web consultant, and you should at least know how to calculate them and how they're used to determine a project's value.

Payback. In its simplest form, you determine the value of a proposal using payback based on how fast you recover the initial cost or investment. If a project recovers its costs before a certain number of years, commonly known as the cutoff level, then it is accepted. A common payback cutoff level is two years. In Proposal D, which costs $5,000, the payback period is somewhere between two and three years. After two years you've made too little ($3,000), and after three years you've more than covered ($6,000) your initial cost. The problem with simply payback is that it does not take into account the time value of money. And even if one were to discount cash flows, you can have two proposals that make the cutoff yet have different NPVs.

IRR. Put simply, IRR is the discount rate that results in a zero NPV. For our example of Proposal D, this is approximately 0.08208209, or 8.2%. This value was determined by trial and error, and you can verify it by plugging it into the equation for Proposal D's NPV (see Figure 4-18).

$$NPV = -\$5,000 + \frac{\$1,000}{(1+r)^1} + \frac{\$2,000}{(1+r)^2} + \frac{\$3,000}{(1+r)^3} = 0$$

Figure 4-18. *For Proposal D, IRR is the value of* r *that makes the NPV = 0;* r *is approximately 8.208209%*

Intuitively, the IRR for a given project is that project's rate of return. Like ROI, companies fix an acceptance rate. If a project's IRR is over the acceptance rate, it is accepted (has high enough value), whereas if it's less than that rate, it is rejected. In practice, IRR and NPV are equivalent, leading to proposals being valued similarly.

In closing, you should now have the techniques needed to quantitatively value your Web site. These techniques are tremendously useful, whether you are a Web entrepreneur trying to decide what kind of Web business to start or a Web consultant trying to convince a client of the value of your proposed Web site. We will use these techniques again in the Web Business Engineering chapters dealing with the analysis and treatment of business processes.

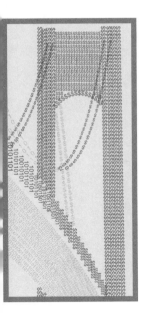

Web Business Engineering: A Quick Primer

The first section of this book prepared you—as a Web entrepreneur or Web consultant—for Web Business Engineering by outlining how different businesses worked together to create a product. We can now see that the Web is far more than just "electronic paper" and have a broad overview of different places and ways a business can effectively use the Web. However, more specific, value-adding ways to use the Web require detailed knowledge of the activities that go on within and between businesses. Acquiring such knowledge requires techniques for analyzing business activities. Web Business Engineering is such a technique. It consists of four steps: (1) mapping business activities, (2) modeling activity value, (3) diagnosing problems or opportunities, and (4) designing treatments. Web Business Engineering is based on the principle that businesses should base their "online" activities on "offline" opportunities if they want to use the Web in a manner that adds value to their organization. An important corollary is that businesses should base their online strategy on offline advantages if they want a sustainable competitive advantage. This section is organized around a case study that highlights these principles and the key steps in Web Business Engineering from a Web consultant's standpoint. Later chapters will present case studies from a Web entrepreneur's perspective.

CHAPTER FIVE

Introduction to Web Business Engineering: Motivation and Basic Principles

Executive Summary

Think of technology without process as similar to knowledge without wisdom. You need the latter to effectively use the former. Web Business Engineering allows you to study *offline* processes so that you can effectively use the Web and other *online* technologies. The basic principle of Web Business Engineering is that businesses should use offline activities to determine online ones, with the important corollary that for a sustainable competitive advantage, businesses need to leverage offline advantages online. Web Business Engineering consists of four steps: (1) mapping business activities, (2) modeling activity value, (3) diagnosing problems and opportunities, and (4) designing treatments. To get you started as quickly as possible, we will not discuss each step in detail but will present a single, in-depth example that highlights the key points and activities of each step. Later sections will present examples that expand upon these steps.

Objectives

After reading this chapter you should be able to:

- *Explain why software-based analysis techniques can be ineffective when used to analyze business activities*

- *Justify the principles underlying Web Business Engineering*

- *Distinguish between information and content*

- *Describe the four steps in Web Business Engineering*

- *Explain why a business's online strategy should be based on offline advantages*

Introduction

Being an expert in all the various Web technologies like HTML, Java, and databases is not sufficient for developing effective business Web sites, nor is it enough to just know how businesses work. Designing effective business Web sites requires the ability to *link* your technical knowledge with business-specific knowledge, the latter of which includes an in-depth understanding of either the strategic objectives and operational details of your client's business (if you're a Web consultant) or of the industry in which you plan to start your Web business (if you're a Web entrepreneur). Without business-specific knowledge driving your designs, you risk creating Web sites that contain a hit-and-miss combination of good and bad features. Some features may have high business value, and others will be superfluous, adding little or no value. For example, a Web site that emphasizes pretty colors, graphics, and layout over functionality may win artistic design awards but fail miserably in terms of generating revenues or cuttings costs for your client's or your own business. When designing a *business* Web site, you must emphasize *value* above all other factors. Aesthetics are still important, but a business Web site's aesthetics are just one of several value-adding factors.

Linking technical with business-specific knowledge requires a technique that allows you to analyze a business's activities, or *processes,* and derive a plan based on those business processes that makes explicit where and how Web technology can be most effectively used in a business. This technique is *Web Business Engineering.* And a Web business engineer is a person that uses Web Business Engineering to design Web sites.

Definition: Web Business Engineering

To get a general idea of what Web Business Engineering is, let us examine the similarities and differences between Web Business Engineering and the closest related activity: business process reengineering. In his book, *Information System*, S. Alter defines a business process as: *a related group of steps or activities that use people, information, and other resources to create value for internal or external resources.*

Business process reengineering is an activity where someone—typically a manager—changes a business process to use different steps or activities, which implies using different people, information, and other resources. In short, the aim of business process reengineering is to develop a new business process that is better along some dimension, such as reducing cost or increasing quality, and then replace an old or stale business process with this new process.

Business engineering and business process reengineering both involve analyzing business processes. However, a key difference between the two is that business process reengineering typically results in *replacing* an existing, inefficient process with a new process. Business engineering, on the other hand, may involve replacing a process, but the primary goal is creating *new* processes that complement, not necessarily replace, existing business processes. Also, unlike business process reengineering, which largely focuses on *eliminating* redundant processes, business engineering can *create* redundant processes, especially when the product of those processes is information (information redundancies are viewed as "good things" in business engineering!). Finally, new businesses, which may not have any business processes in place, can use business-engineering techniques to develop their initial processes based on existing businesses that are similar to their own.

Web Business Engineering can be defined as the analysis of business processes with the goal of creating new processes that make use of the Web—in short, the engineering of business processes that use the Web. These processes may be totally new or may support, extend, or otherwise augment existing processes.

Ways of Studying Business Processes

Popular frameworks used to analyze business processes include data-flow analysis, object-oriented analysis, and entity-relationship models. Many of the frameworks for analyzing business processes are based on analysis methods from the fields of computer science and software engineering. The problem with such frameworks is that they were created with the goal of developing or analyzing computer programs, and for this purpose they have more than demonstrated their usefulness. But part of the reason they are so useful for designing computer programs is the same reason they are inappropriate for designing business processes.

For programmers, these frameworks are useful because there is a close relationship between the framework's units of analysis and the programmer's units of composition. For example, object-oriented analysis depicts problem situations in terms of collections of objects that have methods and properties, and that communicate with each other by exchanging messages across well-known interfaces. There is a very close mapping between the objects, methods, and properties (the units of analysis) depicted in object-oriented analysis and, for example, classes, class member functions, and class variables (the units of composition) in an object-oriented programming language like C++. This tight correspondence between unit of analysis and unit of composition allows programmers to (literally) see and visually explore solutions to the problem—both individually and in group settings—and to readily translate these solutions into implementations—computer programs.

However, for us business managers, consultants, entrepreneurs, and other business analysts, such frameworks present a unit of analysis that is incongruous with our unit of composition. We are used to looking at business problems or opportunities in terms of people that use technology and that follow procedures (people, technology, and procedures are our units of analysis). And we are used to designing solutions to business problems or opportunities that involve new or more people, technology, or procedures (our units of composition). Thus, it is unnatural for us to use techniques that depict business situations as (for example) objects with methods and properties. Consequently, it's more difficult to explore the space of possible solutions as well as more difficult to communicate our solutions with others. Therefore, it is not readily apparent how to translate into implementations the solutions we derive using these computer science–based frameworks.

What we need is a technique that allows us to represent business problems, opportunities, and situations in terms we are familiar with. This will allow us to visually explore the solution space in a manner that leverages our business experience. Whatever technique we use should also make it easy to translate the solutions we discover into designs or implementations that—in our case—use the Web. Finally, the technique should make it easy for us to communicate those solutions to our peers or superiors, such as members of our design team, clients, other managers, and upper management. Web Business Engineering is one such technique that fulfills these requirements.

The Web Business Engineering Framework

To understand Web Business Engineering you need to first understand the principles it is based on.

Web Business Engineering Principle #1: *Work is accomplished by a combination of physical and informational activity.*

Take a product such as the guitar from examples in the last section. A guitar does not magically come into existence; rather the guitar maker first needs to gather the materials that make up the guitar. The guitar maker also needs to come up with designs for how the raw materials should be shaped into finished materials and plans or schedules that describe, among other things, when materials get finished and combined. Once the raw materials and designs/plans are in place, the guitar maker creates the guitar through a combination of physical and informational activity. Specifically, a person or machine following the design (informational activity) shapes the wood (physical activity) into a body and a neck. The design/plan can be written down, memorized, or programmed into a computer, but a person or machine is always following some kind of design and schedule. The neck is then glued or bolted (more physical activity) onto the body, once again following the design (informational activity). Other finished supplies like strings and electronics are then added (yet more physical activity) to the body and neck to complete the guitar, again according to the design. If one were to examine the guitar-making process carefully over time, one would see a constant switching between informational and physical activity (see Figure 5-1). Furthermore, there is not just one activity thread but multiple activity threads—one for each agent, human or machine—involved in the guitar-making process.

In the most general form of business engineering, an analyst studies both physical and informational activities and develops new processes that employ different people, tools, or procedures. Web Business Engineering is a subset of general business engineering, where the focus is on designing new business processes based primarily on an analysis of a business's informational activities. These new processes may employ different people and procedures, but the Web is always a central tool in any newly designed process. This emphasis on analyzing a business's informational activities is a natural consequence of the Web being an information technology.

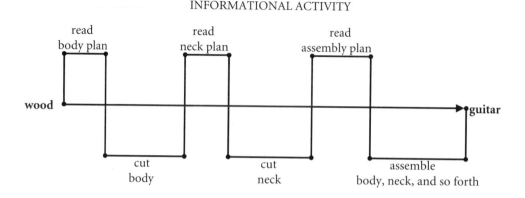

Figure 5-1. *Activity thread showing how informational and physical activities combine to create a guitar*

In Web Business Engineering, the Web is not viewed as a single information technology but rather a collection of online information technologies. Examples include not only Web browsers and applets running in browsers but also technologies not traditionally thought of as part of the Web, such as phones and fax machines. The role of the Web business engineer is to design more effective business processes around a subset of the available online information technologies. The focus on analyzing informational activities brings up the second key principle underlying Web Business Engineering.

Web Business Engineering Principle #2: *Informational/computational work is accomplished by propagating content across media.*

Principle #2 is based on E. Hutchins seminal study of the work processes during large ship navigation. In his studies, Hutchins found that the task of determining where a ship should sail started with someone taking down landmark bearings. The landmark is the initial *content.* This content was propagated to other workers and saved in various *media* (logbook). The workers would change the content and then propagate it down to other workers, who would perform their own content activities, and so on. In Figure 5-2, the bearing taker (BT) uses the alidade to get a direction to a landmark. This direction is verbally relayed to the bearing timer record (BTR), who records the number in a bearing log. The plotter (P) then takes this number and plots it on the map as a line. The culmination of all the content movement and transformation was a record of the ship's current position and a recommendation of where the ship should move next.

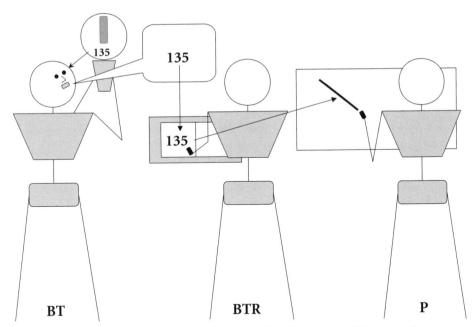

Figure 5-2. *The movement of a landmark bearing across different media*

Businesses accomplish work in a similar fashion by propagating content across media. It is important to note that *content* is not the same thing as *information.* Information consists of two parts: medium and content. For example, a chalkboard with nothing written on it is a medium. The words (content) an instructor writes on the chalkboard denote its content. Together, the chalkboard and the writing constitute information. The distinction between content and its medium is crucial for properly analyzing business processes. After doing a Web Business Engineering analysis one typically finds that certain content is common to both the original and engineered process. What is different is the medium used to store, manipulate, or propagate the content. Thus, this definition of information allows the Web business engineer to separate the variant parts of the system (media) from the invariant aspects of the system (content), the utility of which will be demonstrated in later chapters.

Business Principles

The first two principles structure *how* the Web business engineer analyzes business activities or processes. The last two principles guide *which* processes the analyst engineers for the Web.

Web Business Engineering Principle #3: *Innovative online content can be found by examining offline activities.*

One of the major strengths of the Web is its ability to support all kinds of multimedia. Web sites with just static text and graphics are primitive by today's standards. More advanced Web sites include features such as streamed audio and video, real-time chat rooms, and simulated three-dimensional virtual worlds. Furthermore, the Web's open architecture makes it easy to add new kinds of interactive multimedia content in the form of browser plug-ins or embedded applets.

Unfortunately, the term multimedia has come to be associated mainly with computers, the Web, and the online world in general. People forget that the plain, old offline world *is* a multimedia environment. In fact, the offline world is a more complex multimedia environment than even the best computer multimedia environment. The offline world has real-time sound, video, and interactive chats, just like a computer multimedia environment. But the quality of the sound, video, and interactive chats far exceeds that of a computer multimedia environment. The offline world has quite a number of other sensations that computer multimedia environments have yet to duplicate effectively, including smell, taste, and touch. The offline world, therefore, is a great source of ideas for Web content. Instead of just copying what other Web sites are doing, Web consultants, entrepreneurs, and other Web designers need to get in the habit of looking at what is happening offline as a source of inspiration for innovative online ideas. Virtually all current Web content has its basis in activities that occur in the offline world. Take online auctions, a use of the Web that is often cited as innovative. Those auctions were based on real English auctions. Other examples include online purchasing (based on offline credit card purchasing), chat rooms (based on group conversation), and interactive product experts (based on salespeople). In fact, it is difficult to name an innovative use of the Web (online) that is not based on something that has already happened (offline). By basing online content on offline activities, one has a bigger pool of interactive multimedia ideas from which to draw.

The fourth principle underlying Web Business Engineering, and the most important one from a business standpoint, relates to Web strategy.

Web Business Engineering Principle #4: *A business's online strategy should be based on offline advantages.*

From a competitive standpoint this is the most important principle. To understand why, it is important to realize that Web technologies are largely software technologies. As such, they inherit many of the benefits and drawbacks of software. The saying goes that "software manufacturing costs are epsilon [negligible]." A less-known truism is that "software distribution costs are also epsilon," especially considering how easy it is to set up Web sites for downloading software. Thus, the main costs in developing software are research and development, and if one can afford those costs, then one can mass-produce and distribute software. However, the corollary is that if one can afford the research and development costs, one can copy any software package. The questionable status of software patents makes copying someone else's software especially easy. This is a big problem for Web businesses as well.

For example, suppose you decide to set up a Web bookstore. Furthermore, you've read the latest Internet strategy books that tout "convenience," "mass customization," and "building community" as competitive advantages. So you go off and create a "killer" interactive, database-driven Web site, where all purchasing is conveniently done online. Your Web site implements customization by suggesting books based on customer-specified interests, as well as recommending books based on past customer purchases. Finally, to build community, you have chat sessions with authors, as well as online customer book reviews. Does this bookstore make a great online business? Without question. But is such a business safe from competitors? Is it a viable long-term business? The answer is, highly unlikely. Unfortunately, your competitors are the existing offline bookstores. And anything you put on your Web site, they can put on their Web sites. Online purchasing? Easily copied. Book recommendations? Easily copied. Chat sessions with authors? Easily copied. Online customer book reviews? Easily copied. So in essence, you really don't have any sustainable competitive advantage beyond being the first Web bookstore. Your competitors, on the other hand, have many offline advantages that they can exploit, particularly when they start combining their offline bookstores with their online Web sites. Take convenience, which is often cited as one of the big benefits of online book ordering. Much of this convenience is a result of the fast one- to two-day delivery direct to the customer's mailbox. Now suppose one of your competitors ties its (online) Web site to one of its (offline) stores so that orders are placed online but delivery is accomplished as follows. First, the Web site determines the closest bookstore to the customer. Next, the bookstore reserves the book so that the customer can pick it up on his or her way home, or if the bookstore is close to the customer's neighborhood, a bike courier will drop it off at the customer's house. Either option reduces delivery times to less than a day, making the competitor's online bookstore more convenient than your own. In short, by using online technology (the Web) to exploit offline advantages (existing bookstores) your competitors can find ways of adding value that you (a strictly online company) cannot compete with. This is just one example, but you can probably think of other ways that bookstores can leverage their offline advantages online.

As a final example of the need for companies to have some kind of offline competitive advantage, consider how quickly Microsoft recaptured the browser market from Netscape. Netscape was the prototypical, purely online company. Its products were Web browsers and Web servers, which were distributed primarily over the Web. Netscape's primary advantage was being the first to market with their browser, and as such they were able to capture significant market share (70 percent) early on. However, this position was not sustainable. Because its products were software products, it was vulnerable to imitation, especially from a large software company like Microsoft. And imitate is exactly what Microsoft did. In addition, Microsoft had an offline advantage it could exploit: its existing line of software products, which included office tools, programming languages, databases, and most importantly, the Windows operating system. These were sophisticated products with prohibitively high research and development costs, especially the Windows operating system. Microsoft's Web strategy seamlessly integrated its (online) Web browsers and Web servers with its existing suite of (offline) software products. This made it easier and more convenient for companies to rapidly develop database-driven Web applications with enterprise-wide information sharing and integration with existing office tools. For Netscape to compete, it would need to come up with the same kind of information infrastructure. Once again, unless a company has an offline advantage that it can exploit online, it is vulnerable to offline competitors. A purely online company cannot exist for long. There *are* online advantages, of course, but most if not all are unsustainable.

To summarize, Web Business Engineering is based on four key principles.

1.   Work is a combination of physical and informational activities.

2.   Informational work is accomplished by propagating content across media.

3.   Innovative online content can be found by examining offline activities.

4.   A business's online strategy should be based on offline advantages.

Using Web Business Engineering, one analyzes how content moves across the various media in a business, according to Principles #1 and #2. The goal of this analysis is to discover offline business processes that can beneficially be handled online, according to Principle #3. For a competitive advantage, a business should place online those processes that exploit offline advantages, per Principle #4.

Basic Steps in Web Business Engineering

Now that we have examined the principles underlying Web Business Engineering, let's look at the four main steps.

1. *Map business activity.* In this initial step, the Web business engineer depicts a business in terms of the movement of information across people and technology. The result is a map of informational activity, or an *information activity map.*

2. *Model activity value.* The information activity map from Step 1 is used to create a model of the activity's value. The *value model* is a computational one, which the Web business engineer uses to experiment with different "what-if" scenarios.

3. *Diagnose problems and opportunities.* The value model is used to identify variables in the activity that either drive costs and need to be eliminated or that add high value and need to be supported.

4. *Design treatments.* With problems and opportunities identified, the Web business engineer goes back to the information activity map and uses it to design Web "treatments," uses of the Web that eliminate bad factors or support good ones.

The remaining chapters in this section demonstrate the application of these steps to an actual situation.

CHAPTER SIX

Quick Primer: Step 1, Map Business Activities

Executive Summary

When applying Web Business Engineering, your first step is to create *information activity maps,* maps of specific information activities in a business or industry. One of the key purposes of these maps is to help you explore the space of possible Web solutions. The later steps in Web Business Engineering either directly use or are strongly influenced by the quality of the maps you create. Therefore, it is important to create good information activity maps. This chapter first describes the graphical notation used to create information activity maps and then explains how to apply the notation to map business activities. The chapter ends with an example of mapping an actual business activity. The example is primarily aimed at Web consultants, but is relevant for Web entrepreneurs as well. Later sections in this book will present examples targeted more toward Web entrepreneurs.

Objectives

After reading this chapter you should be able to:

- *Distinguish between business and information activity maps, BAMs versus IAMs*
- *Describe the components of an activity map*
- *Map the information activities in a business*

Introduction

Mapping business activities is the most important step in Web Business Engineering. The output of the mapping stage is what I call a "business activity map," or BAM, for short. A BAM graphically depicts the movement and transformation of materials and information between the various agents—people, technology, and other instruments—that participate in a business or work activity. Because our interest lies mainly in discovering ways of using the Web to support business activities, and the Web is an *information* technology, we will primarily be focusing on a particular kind of business activity map known as an "informational activity map," or IAM, for short. An IAM primarily depicts information as opposed to physical activity in a business. Unless needed we will simply use the term "activity map" throughout.

Activity maps help us explore the space of possible Web solutions to business problems or opportunities. The key word is *explore.* Think of activity maps as analogous to road maps. A road map helps you get from point A to point B, such as from San Diego to Pittsburgh. The map doesn't tell you *how* to get from San Diego to Pittsburgh; it merely shows all the different roads and highways you can take to get there, and you have to pick the best way. Similarly, a business activity map won't tell you how to best use the Web, but it will show you all the different places in a business where you can use the Web to support a work activity. It's up to you to choose the best solution.

The later steps in Web Business Engineering focus on finding good solutions to using the Web in a business, and these steps are either directly or strongly influenced by the map(s) you create, so you want to create good activity maps. Using our road map analogy, a map of the major freeways in the United States may tell you how to get from San Diego to Pittsburgh, for example, but if you want to get from Clairemont (a suburb in San Diego) to La Jolla Shores (a beach in San Diego), then such a map is too high level. A city-level map is needed to figure out a good route. Similarly, certain types of business problems may require you to build a detailed map before you can find solutions, while other types of problems can be solved with a less detailed map. Thus, the quality of your activity map is critical to finding good Web solutions to business problems and opportunities. In the following section, we explore the mapping notation and examine the application of mapping to an actual business situation.

Mapping Notation

Maps have symbols or notations for depicting items that are helpful to the map user. For example, among other things, a city road map depicts streets, highways, and landmarks for drivers. Streets may be indicated by thin black lines with a label parallel to the line denoting the street name. Highways may be labeled similarly but distinguished from streets by a heavy black line. Landmarks can be represented by circles, triangles, squares, and other geometric figures. Similarly, business activity maps have a standard notation for depicting items of interest to Web business engineers.

In Web Business Engineering, the choice of what you annotate in your activity map is based on the principles that (1) work gets accomplished by a combination of physical and informational activities involving people and technology (Principle #1), and (2) informational work is the storing, manipulation, and propagation of content across media (Principle #2; see previous chapter for an explanation of these principles). These principles suggest that the activity map's notation should represent the following:

- Physical goods, or *materials*

- Information

- The *transformation* of materials and information and the *movements* of the results

- People and technology, or *agents*, that participate in a given work activity

In coming up with a notation, we have several goals. First, we need a notation that makes it easy for us to depict these four items as a map of business activity. Second, the resulting activity maps should be easy to understand for you, your team members (if any), and, if you're consulting, your clients. And finally, the notation should allow us to readily and visually explore the space of possible Web solutions, similar to the way a map allows one to explore possible routes to a destination.

Depicting Materials and Information

Materials. You denote materials by a label followed by a colon (material:). For example, take the raw materials used to build a guitar, such as the wood and electronics. In an activity map, those materials would be represented as shown in Figure 6-1.

wood:

electronics:

Figure 6-1. *Notations used to depict materials*

Information. In the previous chapter, information was defined as a *medium* containing some kind of *content*. Note that a medium is always some physical or material thing. So in line with our notation for depicting materials, you denote a medium as a label followed by a colon (medium:). Conversely, you denote content as a colon followed by a label (:content). Information combines the notation for medium and content (medium:content). For example, imagine you're a guitar maker and you have information in the form of paper plans for building a guitar's body and neck. You would depict this information as shown in Figure 6-2.

paper: body plans

paper: neck plans

Figure 6-2. *Notations used to depict information*

Now let's look at how to depict the people and tools that transform and distribute materials and information.

Depicting Agents, Movement, and Transformations

Business activities involve people and technologies, or *agents,* transforming materials and information to create goods or provide services. The term *technology* is a broad one, and you shouldn't take it to mean just high-tech or information technology. For example, a simple file cabinet is a technology agent in Web Business Engineering. During the transformation process, agents receive materials or information from other (downstream) agents, *transform* these items, and then *distribute* them to other (upstream) agents. This process continues for some time, eventually culminating in a product. We just saw how materials and information are denoted. In this section we look at how to denote agents, transformations, and the movement of information and materials.

Agents. In Web Business Engineering, you depict agents as labels with boldfaced type. So, for instance, the person that builds the guitar bodies in our guitar maker example is denoted simply as **body builder**. Similarly, the person who builds the neck for our guitar is denoted as **neck builder**.

Movement, or distribution, of materials and information. Whenever you have a distribution of materials or information from one agent to another, you depict that movement with an arrow between the agents; the arrowhead points toward the agent that receives the item. The arrow is labeled with the information or material that the agents exchange. Figure 6-3 depicts the situation where a body builder and neck builder give their parts to an assembler.

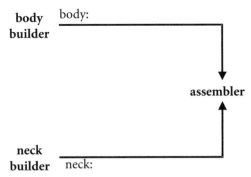

Figure 6-3. *The movement of materials between agents*

Transformations. There is no special notation for describing a transformation. The arrows going into and out of an agent denote the transformation. The labels on the arrows going into an agent denote the materials or information that is about to be transformed, and the labels on the arrows going out of an agent denote the transformed item. Figure 6-4 depicts the assembler creating a guitar out of a body and a neck.

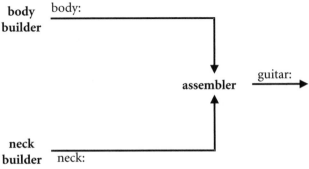

Figure 6-4. *A transformation of materials*

Example. So now we have all the pieces needed to make a business activity map. Let's look at an example to see how everything fits together. Suppose building a guitar requires three individuals: two builders that shape the wood into the guitar's body and neck and an assembler that takes the guitar body, neck, and electronics and assembles them into the final guitar. Further suppose that the builders and assembler are inexperienced and still refer to designs (on paper) to help them do their jobs. Using the Web Business Engineering mapping notation, you would depict the activity of building a guitar as shown in Figure 6-5.

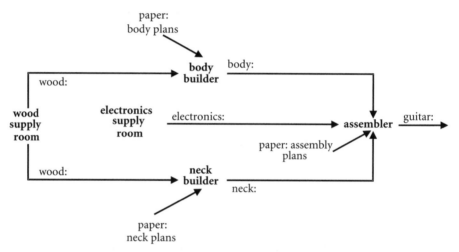

Figure 6-5.   *An activity map for building a guitar*

Figure 6-5 includes two agents that were not part of the initial description of the guitar building process: the wood supply room and the electronics supply room where the builders and assemblers get the materials they need to do their jobs. Their inclusion is a natural consequence of mapping business activities; the act of mapping forces you to be explicit about all the agents that participate. Raw materials and information do not just appear; there must be some agent responsible for their existence. So our finished map typically has more details than we initially expected.

Diagram Scope. A question I'm often asked is "What is the scope of a business activity map?" There are two answers, a short one and a long one. The short answer is that *you start with supplies and end with a product,* where the supplies and product can be either informational, as in a service, or material, as in a physical good. Unfortunately, this answer begs the question "Who supplies the suppliers?" For instance, in Figure 6-5, wood is shown coming out of a wood supply room. But don't wood suppliers stock wood to the supply room? Shouldn't they be depicted in the map?

This brings up my long answer to the original scope question: "It depends." Remember that you, as a Web business engineer, are trying to solve a business problem, and the activity map is but one of the tools you use in your analysis. If after the full analysis you don't come up with a solution, then you may need to do several things, one of which is increasing the scope of your activity map. This is no different from any other methodology. For example, in object-oriented design, if your object diagrams don't give you the information you need to start implementing your computer program, you increase their scope and detail.

An Information-Intensive Example

The previous example illustrated how you used the mapping notation to depict a business process that combined raw materials with information. However, the information in our example was all paper based—the body, neck, and assembly plans. To illustrate the mapping notation on a more information-intensive process that uses different media, take the example of a manager who wants to send a thank you letter to a friend. To send this letter, the manager first looks in a Rolodex for the friend's address. The manager then verbally relays the address and the thank you message to a secretary. The secretary, in turn, manually writes the thank you message on paper as well as the address on the envelope. He or she then puts the letter into an envelope, puts a stamp on the envelope, and finally drops the letter into a mailbox. The postal service then takes the letter and delivers it to the manager's friend. Using the mapping notation we just saw, this situation would appear as in Figure 6-6.

However, this notation can get tedious particularly when mapping many activities within the same business. The following conventions (which I use) may be helpful: Denote all agents as upper-case letters in boldface type, and denote all representations and physical goods that move between agents as lower-case letters with the actual content or type of physical good spelled out. You would then depict the diagram as shown in Figure 6-7.

Note that you can easily draw these maps by hand, on paper, or on a chalk-board. You can also use any number of popular drawing packages, since almost all drawing packages support labels and arrows.[1] The notation is very rich and capable of depicting virtually any business activity. Again, these diagrams are not data

---

[1]The program I used to create the diagrams in this book was Microsoft™ PowerPoint 2000™. One nice feature of this program is the ability to automatically connect labels with arrows so they move together as one group.

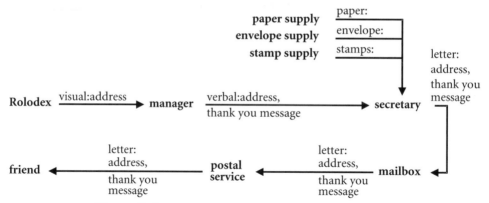

Figure 6-6.   *Mapping notation for a mailing situation*

flow diagrams that depict the movement of information between processes. Rather, these diagrams depict the actual movement of information and materials between the actual agents that participate in a work activity. This level of abstraction allows you to easily see different ways of using the Web to support an activity by substituting the Web for the agents or media in the map. This topic will be covered in more detail in Chapter 9. Next, let see how to apply mapping to a real business situation.

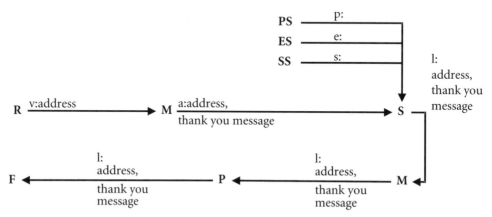

Figure 6-7.   *Shorthand notation for the mailing example; note only content is spelled out*

The Employee Distance Education Case (EDEC)

In business schools, instructors commonly teach new concepts using "cases." Cases are past business situations where the concepts or techniques the instructor is teaching have been successfully applied. The goal is for students to explore various solutions—there can be more than one "answer" to a business case—without having to worry about the consequences of making a bad decision (except for a bad grade!). Similarly, to illustrate the concepts and techniques in Web Business Engineering, we'll look at an actual case where I applied them to successfully solve a business problem.[2] We'll use this case throughout the next couple of chapters, so pay careful attention to the details. Note once again that this case is mainly relevant to Web consultants. However, if you're a Web entrepreneur, you should be able to easily adapt the ideas presented for your own use. And don't worry—we *will* cover case studies targeted at Web entrepreneurs in later chapters.

Business Case: The Employee Distance Education Program

The Mental Systems Corporation[3] is a large hi-tech company with offices spread across the country. Mental Systems places a premium on employee training and education and offers its employees both individual courses and certificate programs that cover a variety of different technical and management topics. Because its employees are geographically spread out, Mental Systems created an Employee Distance Education Center, appropriately nicknamed EDEC, to broadcast real-time instruction to employees located at the satellite offices. EDEC is run as a profit-center, which is a department or business unit that is a part of some larger company but is treated as a separate business—with revenues and costs—so that profitability can be measured.

One of EDEC's most popular offerings is the Certificate in Management program, which all employees must take if they want to move into a management position. However, EDEC's director is concerned because the operating costs for this program are extremely high. One cost that stands out in particular is the mailing costs for homework assignments and readings, which the director feels is an unnecessary expense given technologies like the Web that can distribute the same material electronically. So, the director hires you as a consultant to help him figure out how to use the Web to reduce these mailing costs. The EDEC director supplies the following information about the program:

---

[2]The names in this case have been changed to preserve anonymity.
[3]This is a fictitious name. Any resemblance to an existing or past company is purely coincidental.

- The "Certificate in Management" program runs three years.

- Each year is divided into six minisemesters of seven weeks each.

- Four courses are taught each minisemester, twice a week.

- Students take classes part time at night.

- The lectures are broadcast to six different sites across the country.

- Each site can have from 1 to 20 students.

- Although in-class instruction is broadcast using the latest videoconferencing technology, out-of-classroom activities such as assignments are handled using paper-based mail.

- Paper mailings for the Certificate in Management program are approximately $100,000 per year.

- EDEC's yearly revenues are $1,000,000.

- With the exception of tests, the EDEC's director would like all instructional material placed online. However, the EDEC instructors argue that mail is relatively cheap and the cost of converting paper-based information to a Web-based format is prohibitive.

The remainder of this chapter and the next two chapters demonstrate how you apply Web Business Engineering to determine the best way of using the Web to solve the mailing cost problem in EDEC's Certificate in Management program.

Step 1: Map Business Activity

Before you can draw a road map for some area, it goes without saying that you need details about the various roads in that area. Similarly, before you can map a business activity, you need to know details about that business activity. There are two ways you can obtain these details. The first is through observation. You go to the business and observe the activities of interest, writing down a detailed account of all the information and physical activities that take place during either the creation of a product or the providing of a service. Second, you can interview the managers and employees involved in the activities of interest. Be forewarned, however, that the latter way provides a less-reliable account of what actually happens. People are notorious for giving best case or normative versions of how their work ought to get done, while leaving out many important details of how it actually gets done. You are interested in getting the details of how work *really* gets accomplished.

Suppose EDEC's manager tells you that there are two main kinds of mailings: (1) the instructors mailing students homework assignments and readings and (2) the students mailing back the completed assignments to the instructor. You then interview and observe several instructors, which reveals the following mailing procedure: The instructor gives a paper copy of the assignment to his or her assistant. The assistant makes copies of the assignment and puts them in different Mail Express envelopes, one Mail Express envelope per site. Mail Express delivers the assignments to mail rooms at each of the different sites. Finally, the students get their assignments from the mail room. You can draw the activity map for this procedure in Figure 6-8.

Next you interview the students. You find that similar to mailing assignments, the same agents are involved in returning completed assignments; the primary difference is the type and direction of the information. Specifically, your interviews reveal the following activity: After completing their homework assignments, students place them in a Mail Express package located in their company's mailing room. Later in the day, Mail Express picks up the package and delivers it to the instructor's assistant at EDEC. The assistant opens the package and slips the completed assignments under the instructor's door. You can draw the activity map for this procedure as in Figure 6-9.

Finally, you can represent the entire mailing activity on one diagram by combining the two activity maps; to indicate the sequence of activities, you can

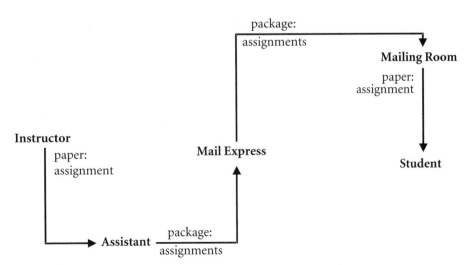

Figure 6-8. *Business activity map for mailing student assignments*

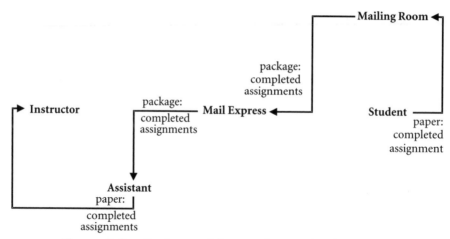

Figure 6-9.   *Business activity map for completed assignments*

number the materials/information with the order in which they are distributed
(see Figure 6-10).

As you can see, these maps are very easy to create by hand. Armed with pencil
and paper, you can simultaneously draw these maps as you interview people or
observe activities. So the next question is "How do we use these maps?" The key is
to note that *any agent or medium on the map is a possible place where the Web can
be applied.* Chapter 9 will cover how to do this in detail; for the remainder of this

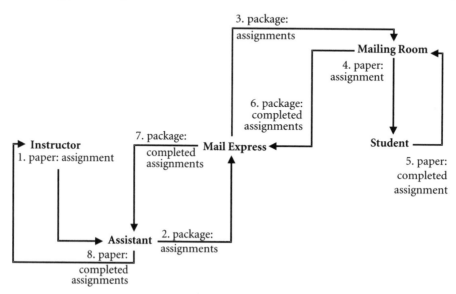

Figure 6-10.   *Composite business activity map for both the student
assignments and completed assignments*

chapter, let's just get an intuitive sense of how you use an activity map to explore the different possible Web solutions.

Using the Activity Map to Explore Possible Web Solutions

There are five agents in the business activity map for the EDEC mailing assignments: instructor, assistant, Mail Express, mailing room, and student. Besides the instructor and student, you can potentially substitute the Web for each agent (see Figure 6-11). In fact, even the instructor may be replaced by some form of totally Web-based instruction! This is what's nice about the activity map; it forces you to look at and consider solutions that might be dismissed offhand.

Instead of replacing a single agent, the Web can be used to replace pairs of agents. For example, the Web can be used to replace both the assistant or Mail Express and the mailing room (see Figure 6-12).

Similarly, one can group Mail Express and the mailing room or the assistant and mail room as possible candidates for Web support (not shown). A final alternative is to replace all intermediate agents (Figure 6-13). Once again, the map allows us to visually explore these different solutions.[4]

In closing, if our goal is merely to discover different ways of using the Web to support a business activity, then the activity map alone is sufficient for that

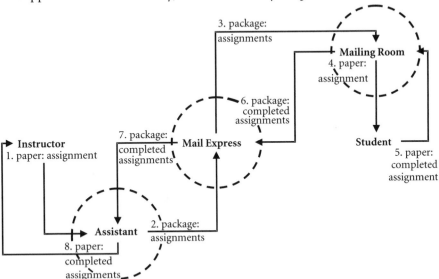

Figure 6-11. *Single-agent Web substitutions*

---

[4]Altogether, given N agents, there are $\sum_{i=1}^{N}\binom{N}{i}$ Web substitutions! For example, given 5 agents ($N = 5$), there are 31 different ways to use the Web by substituting it for different combinations of agents.

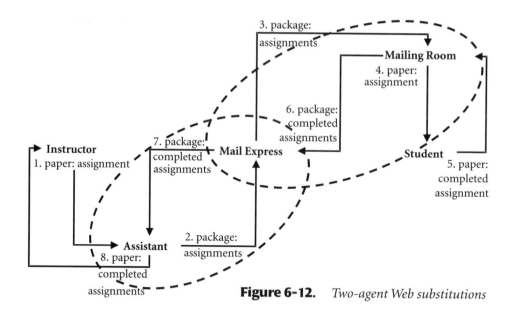

Figure 6-12.   *Two-agent Web substitutions*

purpose. However, if our goal is to find *good* ways of using the Web, solutions that add value—by cutting costs or generating revenues—to a business activity, then we need more than just the activity map. We need some way of valuing the activities in the map so that as we explore different Web solutions, we can determine

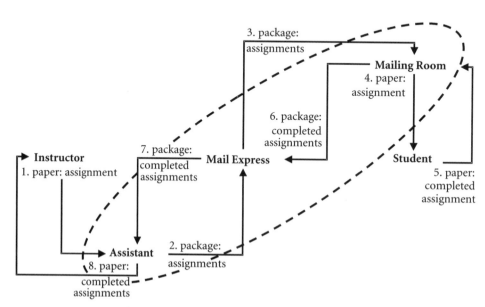

Figure 6-13.   *Three-agent Web substitutions*

their effects and choose the solution that adds the most value. Think of a road map that is *not* drawn to scale. That map will help you find different routes from a starting point to a destination point. But unless the map is drawn to scale or the roads in the map are annotated with their length (for example, in miles), you won't be able to pick the best route or even a good route. Similarly, by valuing our activity map we are able to pick good Web solutions. The next chapter shows you how to create a value model for a business activity that is based on the activity map created in Step 1.

CHAPTER SEVEN

Quick Primer: Step 2, Model Activity Value

Executive Summary

The business activity map shows you the various places where you can use the Web to support an activity in a business or industry. However, the map alone indicates *too many* ways of using the Web, not all of them good. To narrow down the possibilities to just the good Web solutions, you need another tool—a *value model,* which is derived from the activity map. As the name implies, the value model simulates the value of a business activity or map. The model helps you both identify problem areas in an activity and predict the value effects of different Web solutions. There are many different kinds of value models. One is the interaction-cost model, which measures the cost of an information exchange between the agents that participate in a business activity. This chapter shows you how to build an interaction-cost model, and in the next chapter you will learn how to use your model to diagnose problem areas that can benefit from Web "treatments."

Objectives

After reading this chapter you should be able to:

■ *Explain why you need more than the business activity map to help you find good Web solutions*

■ *Build an interaction-cost model based on the business activity map you created in Step 1*

Introduction

Business activity maps depict the distribution, transformation, and storage of materials and information by the people, tools, and other agents that participate in some work activity. The maps provide a useful starting point for exploring different ways of using the Web to support the activity depicted in your map. However, like a road map that shows many different routes to the same destination, not all the different ways of using the Web are equal in terms of value. Your role as a Web business engineer is to determine which activities should be kept offline and which ones should be handled online. The business activity maps alone, however, do not provide the information necessary to make such decisions. You need to use another tool, a value model—which you derive from your activity map—to help you trim down the set of all possible Web uses to just the good ones. As the name implies, the value model calculates the value of the information activities in your map. The model allows you to experiment with different changes to the activity map and to see the (value) effects of those changes in real time. This ability to simulate the effects of hypothetical changes allows you to rate and rank the various ways of using the Web suggested by your activity map.

This chapter shows you how to build a particular kind of value model known as an interaction-cost model. To build this model, you'll use the activity map and other information from the case introduced in the last chapter. In the next chapter you'll learn how to combine your value model with your activity map to identify good ways of using the Web.

Valuing a Business Activity

Business activity maps depict how individuals, technologies, and other agents interact as they transform and distribute materials and information. But these interactions are not free. Costs are associated with each manipulation and movement of materials and information between agents—that is, every arrow in an activity map has a cost associated with it. By adding together these interaction costs you get the cost of the entire activity. This total cost is a measure of the activity's *value*. The idea is that since the business bears those costs, the activity is worth *at least* that much to the organization. However, even if activity costs are not an exact measure of value, the resulting model is usually sufficient for diagnostic purposes. To summarize, one way to calculate the value of an activity is by determining the cost of each individual interaction and then adding them all up. This collection of interaction costs constitutes an *interaction cost model*. Before we look at how to build an entire interaction cost model, you first need to learn how to determine the cost of a single interaction.

Background: What's the Cost of a Single Interaction?

To understand the different kinds of costs in an interaction, let's consider this situation. Suppose a boss scribbles a thank you message on a piece of paper and gives that paper to his or her secretary to type. You would depict this interaction in an activity map like the one in Figure 7-1.

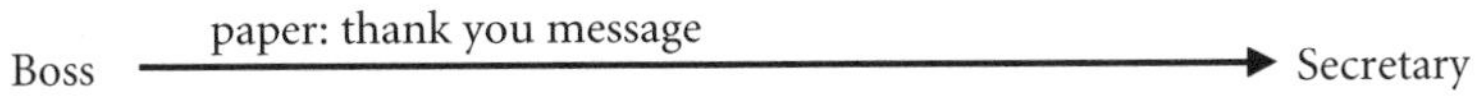

Boss ——————— paper: thank you message ———————▶ Secretary

Figure 7-1. *A simple interaction*

There are several costs implicit in this simple exchange. First, there is the cost of the paper itself, a *material* cost. Second, there is the cost of the boss thinking of a message and writing it up, or a *production* cost; after all, those activities take time, and in businesses, time is money. And finally, there is the cost of delivering the message to the secretary, or a *distribution* cost. There is another kind of cost that doesn't take place in this particular example but deserves mention: *storage* costs, which are any costs incurred with storing the materials or information involved in the interaction.

Therefore, a single interaction contains at least the following four different kinds of costs:

- *Material cost*—the cost of the actual goods exchanged in an interaction
- *Production cost*—the cost of transforming the materials
- *Distribution cost*—the cost of delivering the materials to a new agent
- *Storage cost*—the cost of holding materials

These four costs are direct ones; the interaction cost model tracks *ongoing* activity costs because, typically, those are the ones a business can control. You do not account for sunk costs, such as the costs already incurred for equipment. One cost that should be accounted for, if you have enough data to calculate it, is opportunity cost. This is the cost of not doing something else—for example, the time the boss spends writing thank you messages costs the business because he or she could be spending that time more wisely doing management activities. However, opportunity costs can be difficult to quantify, and I recommend doing so only if the final interaction cost model, based on direct costs, doesn't reveal any solutions.

Now that we know how to model the cost of a single interaction, let's try to model the interaction costs of an entire activity.

Case (Continued): Building an Interaction Cost Model for the EDEC Assignment Mailings

In the last chapter we built an activity map that depicted EDEC instructors mailing homework assignments to students and students mailing back completed assignments (see Figure 7-2). We will now take that activity map and use it as the basis for building an interaction-cost model, which consists of the following five steps:

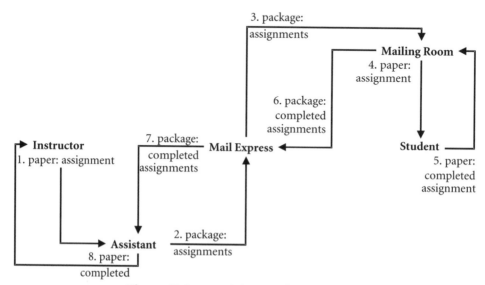

Figure 7-2.   *Activity map from Chapter 6*

1. Determine agents

2. Build the interaction matrix

3. Derive interaction-cost equations

4. Program the interaction-cost equations into the interaction matrix

5. Add summaries

Step 1. Determine Agents

The first step in building an interaction-cost model is determining which agents to include in the model. You do not automatically include all agents in the activity map, only those with interaction costs that the organization must incur. To demonstrate this, let's take a look at the five agents in the EDEC example.

1. Instructor *(I)*, who gives out the homework assignment

2. Assistant *(A)*, in charge of mailing and delivering homework to students and instructors

3. Mail Express *(M)*, the delivery service

4. The mailing room *(R)*, which temporarily holds the Mail Express packages

5. Student *(S)*

The instructor and assistant are employees of EDEC, so they are included in the interaction-cost model. Mail Express is included since EDEC must pay for the mailings. Similarly, the mailing room is included because EDEC reimburses it for packaging the students' assignments and mailing them off to Mail Express. The only agent with costs that EDEC does not pay for are the students. So all agents except the students are included in the model.

Step 2. Build the Interaction Matrix

With the key agents selected, your next step is to create an interaction matrix. In this matrix, the rows indicate the agent that produces and distributes the materials or information (depicted in the activity map by the agent at the base of an arrow), and the columns indicate the agent that receives the transformed materials or information (depicted in the map by the agent at the tip of an arrow).

For our EDEC example, you would create an interaction matrix that looks like Figure 7-3.

INTERACTION MATRIX:

FROM/TO	I	A	M	R
I		$ 5.85		
A	$ 2.75		$ 123.30	
M		$ 1.25		
R			$ 120.00	

Figure 7-3.   *Interaction matrix for our mailing example*

Create this interaction matrix using a spreadsheet package.[1] Each cell in the interaction matrix denotes a particular interaction—a particular arrow in the map. For example, the cell associated with the instructor giving an assignment to an assistant—the arrow labeled "1. paper: assignment" in Figure 7-2—is the cell whose row is *I* and whose column is *A*.

Step 3: Derive Interaction-Cost Equations

Just as each cell in your interaction matrix is associated with a particular interaction (or arrow in the map), the value inside a given cell represents the cost of that interaction. You do not hard-code these values. Rather, you derive and program an equation that represents the cost, and the output of that equation is what shows up in the cell. We'll look at how to create these interaction-cost equations, but first note that not all cells in the interaction matrix are used. For example, the activity map does not show the instructor *(I)* delivering packages directly to Mail Express *(M)*. Instead, *I* gives the assistant *(A)* the assignments, who then makes copies before sending them to *M*. Thus, the cost of *I* interacting with *M* is zero, and that cell is left blank. Because *A* does interact with *M*, the corresponding cell will hold an equation representing the interaction cost.

The Cost of the Instructor $\rightarrow$ Assistant Interaction

Virtually all the EDEC instructors have their assignments stored electronically in their computers and simply print them out. Thus, the production cost for an assignment is simply the cost of the instructor's time printing out the document. You can denote this cost as the instructor's hourly wage (IWAGE) multiplied by the time spent printing the document (PTIME):

$$\textit{Production Cost (Assignment)} = \text{IWAGE} \times \text{PTIME}$$

---

[1] I use Microsoft Excel™, but any package that allows you to program equations into cells will do.

The materials cost is the number of pages in the assignment (NPAGES) multiplied by the cost per page (CPAGE). Although assignments can vary in terms of number of pages, we can simplify the equation by using the average number of pages in an assignment:

$$Materials\ Cost = \text{NPAGES} \times \text{CPAGE}$$

The distribution cost for the assignment is simply the time it takes the instructor to walk over to the assistant's office and drop off the paper assignment (DTIME):

$$Distribution\ Cost = \text{IWAGE} \times \text{DTIME}$$

In summary, the cost of the instructor-assistant interaction is the sum of the production costs, materials cost, and distribution costs:

$$I \rightarrow A: \ \text{IWAGE} \times \text{PTIME} + \text{NPAGES} \times \text{CPAGE} + \text{IWAGE} \times \text{DTIME}$$

The Cost of the Assistant $\rightarrow$ Mail Express Interaction

In the assistant $\rightarrow$ Mail Express interaction, the assistant makes copies of the assignment, places these in a Mail Express package, and drops them off at a Mail Express mailbox. The production cost is the cost of copying the assignment, which is the time it takes the assistant to make and package the copies (CTIME) multiplied by the assistant's hourly wage (AWAGE):

$$Production\ Cost\ (Copies) = \text{AWAGE} \times \text{CTIME}$$

The materials cost is the cost of the paper (CPAGE) on which the assignment is copied. All pages of the assignment (NPAGES) need to be copied for as many students as there are in the class (NSTUD). Thus, the materials cost is:

$$Materials\ Cost = \text{NSTUD} \times \text{NPAGES} \times \text{CPAGE}$$

The copies are split into several piles that correspond to the different remote sites (NSITES). Each pile is put in a different Mail Express envelope, which has a mailing fee associated with it (MAILXFEE) that varies depending on how fast the instructor needs the assignment delivered—for example, overnight versus two days. Part of the distribution cost is this mailing cost (MAILXFEE × NSITES); the other is the cost of the time it takes the assistant to drop off packages at the Mail Express mailbox (MTIME × AWAGE).

$$\textit{Distribution Cost} = \text{MAILXFEE} \times \text{NSITES} + \text{MTIME} \times \text{AWAGE}$$

So to summarize, the cost of the $A \longrightarrow M$ interaction is:

$$\textbf{\textit{A}} \longrightarrow \textbf{\textit{M}}: \text{AWAGE} \times \text{CTIME} + \text{NSTUD} \times \text{NPAGES} \times \text{CPAGE} +$$
$$\text{MAILXFEE} \times \text{NSITES} + \text{MTIME} \times \text{AWAGE}$$

The Cost of the Mail Room $\longrightarrow$ Mail Express Interaction

The result of the $R \longrightarrow M$ interaction is a Mail Express package with the students' homework assignments in it. It is important to emphasize that in determining costs, you only account for the factors that your client (EDEC) has control over—those he or she pays for. In our example, EDEC only pays for the Mail Express fee, not for any other mail-room activity, such as the time spent packaging the assignments. Thus, the only cost incurred by EDEC is the cost of reimbursing each of the sites for the Mail Express packages, a distribution cost. In sum, the cost of the $R \longrightarrow M$ interaction is:

$$\textbf{\textit{R}} \longrightarrow \textbf{\textit{M}}: \text{MAILXFEE} \times \text{NSITES}$$

The Cost of the Mail Express $\longrightarrow$ Assistant Interaction

Mail Express delivers the packages with the completed assignments to the assistant. The only cost in this interaction is the cost of the assistant's time (STIME) spent in receiving the packages:

$$\textbf{\textit{M}} \longrightarrow \textbf{\textit{A:}} \text{AWAGE} \times \text{STIME}$$

The Cost of the Assistant $\longrightarrow$ Instructor Interaction

The assistant *(A)* unpackages the assignments and slips them under the instructor's *(I)* door. The production costs are a function of the time (RTIME) it takes the assistant to remove the individual assignments from each of the Mail Express packages (a total of NSITES packages in all):

$$Production\ Cost = \text{AWAGE} \times \text{RTIME} \times \text{NSITES}$$

There are no material costs. Distribution costs are a function of the time it takes the assistant to deliver the assignments to the instructor. Because assignments usually have a fixed due date, the Mail Express packages from the various sites all arrive on the same day. The assistant unpacks them all and then delivers them as a batch to the instructor. This cost is a function of the time it takes the assistant to walk over to the instructor's office and stick the assignments under the door:

$$Distribution\ Cost = \text{AWAGE} \times \text{WTIME}$$

So the cost of the $A \longrightarrow I$ interaction is:

$$A \longrightarrow I: \text{AWAGE} \times \text{RTIME} \times \text{NSITES} + \text{AWAGE} \times \text{WTIME}$$

Step 4: Program the Interaction-Cost Equations into the Interaction Matrix

Now that you've derived the equations for all the individual interaction costs, the next step is to program these equations into the interaction matrix. Before you do this, however, create a *control panel* that contains all the variables used in the equations. The control panel will be your primary interface during the diagnosis phase. In a spreadsheet, you implement the control panel as a two-column table; the first column contains the variable names and the second column their values (see Figure 7-4). Initially, you fill the value column with the actual activity values.

With the control panel created, you simply fill in the cells of the matrix with the formulas for the various interaction costs. Spreadsheet packages like Microsoft Excel™ make it very easy to enter the formulas. Excel™ allows you to assign any cell a name. Name the cells in the value column their corresponding variable name. This makes programming the interaction cost equations very easy. For example, the $A \longrightarrow M$ interaction is defined as:

$$A \longrightarrow M: \text{AWAGE} \times \text{CTIME} + \text{NSTUD} \times \text{NPAGES} \times \text{CPAGE} + \\ \text{MAILXFEE} \times \text{NSITES} + \text{MTIME} \times \text{AWAGE}$$

```
CONTROL PANEL          units        comment
     IWAGE  $    50.00               per hour
     AWAGE  $    15.00               per hour
     PTIME          0.03 hours       2 minutes
     DTIME          0.08 hours       5 minutes
     CTIME          0.08 hours       5 minutes
     MTIME          0.08 hours       5 minutes
     STIME          0.08 hours       5 minutes
     RTIME          0.02 hours       1 minute
     WTIME          0.08 hours       5 minutes
     CPAGE  $     0.01 per page      1 penny
    NPAGES             2 pages
     NSTUD            40 students
    NSITES             6 locations
  MAILXFEE  $    20.00               overnight
```

Figure 7-4.   *Variable control panel for the mailing example*

To program this equation, you simply go to the cell associated with $A \rightarrow M$ and enter it (see Figure 7-5). The final step is to add summary information to the interaction-cost model.

Step 5: Add Summaries

The final step is to add a summary row to your interaction-cost model. In a spreadsheet, the summary row is simply a row of cells that summarizes the cost of the activity as well as the activity costs spread out both over time and across additional agents. In our example, the interaction matrix contains the costs for a single mailing by a single instructor. At minimum, the summary row should show this single mailing cost, which is calculated as the sum of all the cells in the interaction matrix.

SINGLE = SUM (All Cells in the Interaction Matrix)

Another useful summary cost is the cost of mailings per week for a single instructor. Recall that courses are taught twice a week (TFREQ), so the weekly cost is:

WEEKLY = TFREQ × SINGLE

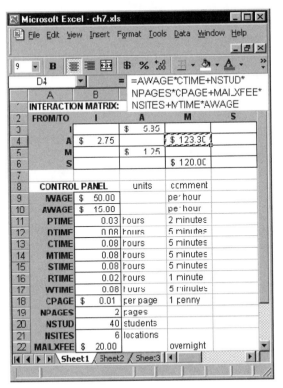

Figure 7-5. *Programming the A → M interaction-cost equation into the interaction matrix*

There are seven weeks (WMINI) in a minisemester, so the minisemester cost for one instructor is:

$$MINI = WMINI \times WEEKLY$$

Four instructors (NINST) teach per minisemester. Across all instructors, the mailing cost is:

$$MINI\_ALL = MINI \times NINST$$

Lastly, there are six minisemesters (NMINI) per year. So the yearly mailing costs across all instructors in EDEC's Certificate in Management Program is:

$$YEARLY = MINI\_ALL \times NMINI$$

Add the extra variables in these cost summary equations to the end of the control panel (see Figure 7-6).

CONTROL PANEL		units	comment
IWAGE	$ 50.00		per hour
AWAGE	$ 15.00		per hour
PTIME	0.03	hours	2 minutes
DTIME	0.08	hours	5 minutes
CTIME	0.08	hours	5 minutes
MTIME	0.08	hours	5 minutes
STIME	0.08	hours	5 minutes
RTIME	0.02	hours	1 minute
WTIME	0.08	hours	5 minutes
CPAGE	$ 0.01	per page	1 penny
NPAGES	2	pages	
NSTUD	40	students	
NSITES	6	locations	
MAILXFEE	$ 20.00		overnight
TFREQ	2		per week
NINST	4		instructors
WMINI	7	weeks	per mini
NMINI	6		per year

Figure 7-6. *The new control panel with variables for the summary row added*

Finally, use these additional variables to program the summary equations into the cells of the summary row similar to the manner in which you programmed the cost equations for the interaction matrix (see Figure 7-7).

SUMMARY

SINGLE	WEEKLY	MINI	MINI-ALL	YEARLY
$253.15	$506.31	$3,544.15	$14,176.59	$85,059.52

Figure 7-7. *Summary of the mailing process*

Your interaction-cost model is now finished! Note it is not necessary to represent the model as separate spreadsheets. You can represent the entire interaction-cost model on one spreadsheet (see Figure 7-8).

One last question remains before we continue: How do you know your model is correct? If correct, the model's yearly mailing costs should be close to EDEC's actual yearly mailing costs, which is $100K. The model's yearly costs are approximately $85K, which is indeed close to EDEC's actual cost. The $15K

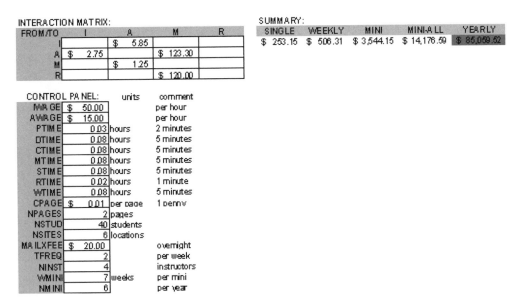

Figure 7-8.   *Interaction-cost model for the EDEC assignment mailings*

difference is likely due to books and other materials that are mailed at the beginning of the minisemester and tests mailed at the end of the minisemester. These
"one-time" costs are not part of the ongoing mailing costs and, thus, were not
incorporated into the interaction-cost model. In general, you verify your model
by comparing its values with the actual values from the activity you modeled; if
they are close, then you probably have a good model, and if not, you need to go
back and fix your value equations. With a correct model, we can now continue to
the diagnostic step.

CHAPTER EIGHT

Quick Primer: Step 3, Diagnose Problems and Opportunities

Executive Summary

After creating the value model, you're ready for diagnosis. The goal of diagnosis is to help you identify those interactions from your activity map that are likely to add the most value when handled online. The primary tool for assisting you in your diagnosis is your value model. The general procedure calls for you to "tweak" your value model's variables and examine the effects of those tweaks on the activity's value. Those tweaks resulting in high value indicate interactions that should be handled online. In this chapter, you learn how to perform diagnosis using the interaction-cost model that you created in the previous chapter. Because your value model is cost-based, increasing value translates into cutting costs. You tweak the variables in your model in an attempt to identify those factors responsible for driving the costs high—cost drivers. The interactions linked to the big cost drivers are potential candidates for online handling. The next chapter will show you how to take your diagnostic findings and design treatments for them.

Objectives

After reading this chapter you should be able to:

- *Explain why diagnosis is better than ad hoc/intuitive guessing*

- *Diagnose business activities using an interaction-cost model*

Introduction

Diagnosis is the step in Web Business Engineering where you identify those parts of a business activity that should be handled online. Think of your diagnosis of business activities as analogous to the medical diagnosis a physician performs on a patient with some unknown illness. The physician runs tests on the patient with the help of various medical instruments. Based on the results of those tests, the physician determines what illness the patient has and recommends treatments. Similarly you, as a Web business engineer, use an instrument (the value model) to run (simulated) tests on a business. The results of your tests indicate problem or opportunity areas in a business, which may benefit from being online. And once these areas are identified, you can start designing treatments: specific solutions that use the Web.

The specific tests you run during diagnosis depend on the type of value model you have. When your value model is an interaction-cost model, your primary goal is to identify the big cost drivers: those factors responsible for significantly driving up activity costs. Thus, the particular tests you run are those that make explicit the variables in your model that play a significant role in increasing costs. Mostly, you'd like to identify variables that, when you reduce their amounts, result in *order of magnitude* cost reductions. The idea is that these variables are linked to interactions in your activity map, and if you can find a way to reduce the cost of these interactions by handling them online (online treatments), then you'll get a corresponding order of magnitude decrease in the overall activity's cost.

In this chapter, we'll focus on diagnosis and leave the online treatments for the next chapter. Unfortunately, in Web Business Engineering "diagnosis" is the least systematic of all the steps. There are no tests *guaranteed* to identify offline interactions that should be handled online, just as there are no procedures that are guaranteed to help a physician correctly diagnose all illness, but there are many heuristic practices that are effective in identifying those interactions.

First, let's look at the basic steps in performing a diagnosis.

1. Identify value drivers. (When the value model is an interaction-cost model, this step is equivalent to identifying cost drivers.)

2. Separate variant from invariant drivers.

3. Determine the effects of realistic changes to the variant drivers.

Once again, we'll use the EDEC case from the previous chapters to illustrate the application of these diagnostic steps.

Case (Continued): Diagnosing the EDEC Mailing Costs

To recap, in the EDEC case you're a consultant hired to reduce EDEC's huge mailing costs by using the Web. You've already created an information activity map and an interaction-cost model that accurately represent the information movement and costs, respectively, for EDEC's "assignment mailings." The activity maps indicate numerous offline interactions that you could handle online, but they don't tell you which ones will provide EDEC the most benefit when handled online. So to help you out, you built a particular kind of value model, known as an interaction-cost model, that accurately models the mailing costs (see Figure 8-1).

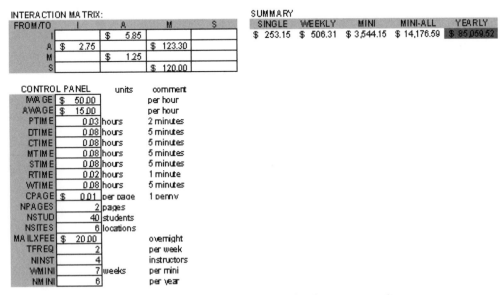

Figure 8-1. *Interaction-cost model for the EDEC mailing case*

Next, you'll use the interaction-cost model to identify the interactions that should be handled online. Keep in mind that the big plan is for you to note variables in the model that significantly drive up costs (cost drivers), identify the interactions associated with these variables, and reduce the cost of those interactions by handling them online, thus significantly reducing the costs of the overall activity.

The Dangers of Intuition and Guessing: The Interaction-Cost Model Versus Common Sense

The cost drivers are not apparent simply from reading the descriptions of the mailing activity or looking at the activity map. The beauty of the interaction-cost model is that it allows you to systematically determine cost drivers instead of just guessing or applying commonsense rules that turn out to be just plain wrong.

For example, one commonsense rule for reducing costs is to eliminate or reduce those factors that cost the most. Let's assume that you are a naive consultant who is not applying Web Business Engineering and you adopt this rule. Looking at the control panel, it is clear that the instructor's wage is very high—$50/hour for an experienced instructor. Suppose you decide that one way to reduce costs is by hiring cheaper labor (again, a commonsense thing to do)—specifically hiring junior instructors at $25/hour. You make this recommendation to EDEC.

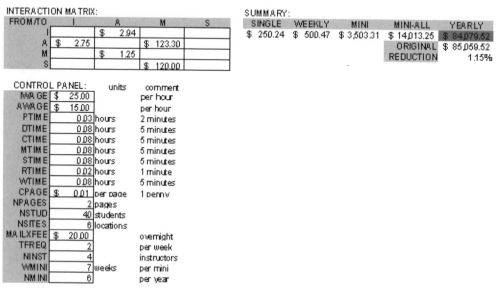

Figure 8-2. *Savings from cutting instructor's wages in half*

How does this action affect mailing costs? Without the model, it is difficult to tell. However, with the model, one can plug in $25/hour for the instructor's wage (IWAGE) and see that there is only about a 1 percent reduction in total cost—1.15% to be precise (see Figure 8-2). (Note: I've modified the summary row of the model to show the reduction.) In short, common sense is wrong in this situation!

Another commonsense rule is to reduce costs by having employees work more efficiently. For example, suppose you, as a naive consultant, believe that if every employee worked twice as fast, costs would be reduced. In the interaction-cost model this would correspond to cutting all the time variables (PTIME, DTIME, CTIME, MTIME, STIME, RTIME, and WTIME) in half. You recommend to EDEC that they order all their employees to work faster. Will working twice as fast result in a significant cost reduction? Nope. The model shows that, at most, EDEC reduces costs by 2.4% (see Figure 8-3).

Yet another common sense rule is to reduce overall costs by reducing supply costs, which in this example would correspond to finding a cheaper supplier for paper. Reducing the costs of paper to one-half penny per page only results in a cost reduction of .16% (not shown). Once again, applying commonsense rules results in very little cost savings. What you need to strive for, as a Web business engineer, are recommendations that result in cost reductions of an order of magnitude or more. This, in turn, requires systematic techniques for making the big cost drivers explicit in your interaction-cost model.

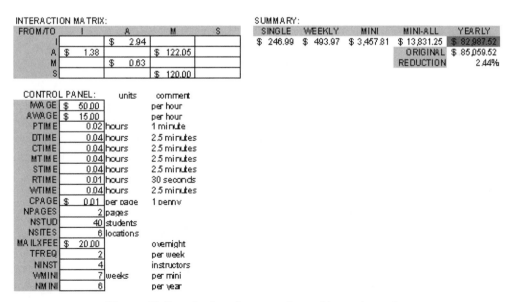

Figure 8-3. *Savings from people working twice as fast*

INTERACTION MATRIX:

FROM/TO	I	A	M	S
I		$ 5.85		
A	$ 2.75		$ 123.30	
M		$ 1.25		
S			$ 120.00	

SUMMARY:

SINGLE	WEEKLY	MINI	MINI-ALL	YEARLY
$ 253.15	$ 506.31	$ 3,544.15	$ 14,176.59	$ 85,059.52
			ORIGINAL	$ 85,059.52
			REDUCTION	0.00%

CONTROL PANEL:

		units	comment	50%
MWAGE	$ 50.00		per hour	1.15%
AWAGE	$ 15.00		per hour	1.28%
PTIME	0.03	hours	2 minutes	0.33%
DTIME	0.08	hours	5 minutes	0.82%
CTIME	0.08	hours	5 minutes	0.25%
MTIME	0.08	hours	5 minutes	0.25%
STIME	0.08	hours	5 minutes	0.25%
RTIME	0.02	hours	1 minute	0.30%
WTIME	0.08	hours	5 minutes	0.25%
CPAGE	$ 0.01	per page	1 penny	0.16%
NPAGES	2	pages		0.16%
NSTUD	40	students		0.16%
NSITES	6	locations		47.70%
MAILXFEE	$ 20.00		overnight	47.40%
TFREQ	2		per week	50.00%
NINST	4		instructors	50.00%
WMINI	7	weeks	per mini	50.00%
NMINI	6		per year	50.00%

Figure 8-4.   *The "one-half heuristic" for determining cost drivers*

Step 1. Identify Value Drivers: The One-half Heuristic

To systematically determine cost drivers, you must tweak the values in the control panel. A simple but powerful heuristic is to cut all variables in half, one at a time, and note the cost reductions. The variables that result in the biggest reductions are the cost drivers. Instead of demonstrating this heuristic on every variable, the results are summarized in Figure 8-4. The interaction-cost model shows that cutting in half the Mail Express fee (MAILXFEE), the number of participating business units (NSITES), the frequency of mailings (TFREQ), the number of instructors in the EDEC program (NINST), the number of weeks in a mini-semester (WMINI), and the number of minisemesters per year (NMINI) results in the greatest savings: 47.40%, 47.70%, 50%, 50%, 50%, and 50%, respectively. Thus, these variables are the big cost drivers. Halving all other variables results in savings of less than 2%, so those other variables are *not* the key cost drivers.

Step 2. Separate the Variant from the Invariant Drivers

Not all cost drivers are created equally. There are certain variables that the organization cannot change for logistical or cultural reasons, among others. You need to separate these invariant cost drivers from the variant cost drivers, the variables that the organization can change. NSITES, NINST, WMINI, and NMINI are all invariant cost drivers. In EDEC's Certificate of Management program, there must be four courses taught per minisemester, and therefore four instructors (NINST) for the program to finish in three years. For similar reasons, the number of weeks in a minisemester (WMINI) as well as the number of minisemesters per year (NMINI) cannot change. Finally, the program must be open to all employees; EDEC cannot restrict employees at different locations from enrolling, so there will always be six participating business units (NSITES).

Thus, the variant cost drivers are the Mail Express fee (MAILXFEE) and the frequency of assignment mailings (TFREQ). For our purposes, let's assume that for cultural reasons EDEC can't restrict the number of assignments mailed per week, so TFREQ is an invariant cost driver. This leaves only the Mail Express fee (MAILXFEE) as the cost driver.

Step 3. Determine the Effects of Realistic Changes

Steps 1 and 2 helped you identify the variant cost drivers. To determine these drivers, you entered unrealistic values into your model—you simply divided each variable amount in half. In Step 3, realistic amounts for the driver variables are entered so that you get a more accurate reading on the cost reductions. This gives you a sense of what would happen if you designed an online treatment that eliminated or reduced the cost driver.

For example, one cost driver is the Mail Express fee (MAILXFEE), which is $20 for overnight delivery. Suppose that instead of Mail Express overnight delivery, the EDEC instructors send their assignments two days early and thus can use two-day mail at $3 per package. Plugging in $3 for MAILXFEE results in a yearly mailing cost of $16,515.52 instead of $85,059.52 (see Figure 8-5)—an 80.58% cost reduction!

You can also try reducing the mailing fees to zero (see Figure 8-6). This gives you a rough idea of what would happen if you put all assignments online. Reducing MAILXFEE to zero results in a yearly mailing cost of $4,419.52, about a 95% reduction in mailing costs. Thus, our model strongly suggests that putting assignments online will result in an order of magnitude reduction in costs.

More precisely, any Web solution that drastically reduces or eliminates the MAILXFEE will result in a reduction of EDEC's mailing costs by an order of magnitude. Having identified the cost drivers and verified that reducing their values will result in significant cost reductions, your next step is to actually design an online solution (treatment) that accomplishes these reductions.

INTERACTION MATRIX:

FROM/TO	I	A	M	S
I		$ 5.85		
A	$ 2.75		$ 21.30	
M		$ 1.25		
S			$ 18.00	

SUMMARY:

SINGLE	WEEKLY	MINI	MINI-ALL	YEARLY
$ 49.15	$ 98.31	$ 688.15	$ 2,752.59	$ 16,515.52
			ORIGINAL	$ 85,059.52
			REDUCTION	80.58%

CONTROL PANEL:		units	comment
WAGE	$ 50.00		per hour
AWAGE	$ 15.00		per hour
PTIME	0.03	hours	2 minutes
DTIME	0.08	hours	5 minutes
CTIME	0.08	hours	5 minutes
MTIME	0.08	hours	5 minutes
STIME	0.08	hours	5 minutes
RTIME	0.02	hours	1 minute
WTIME	0.08	hours	5 minutes
CPAGE	$ 0.01	per page	1 penny
NPAGES	2	pages	
NSTUD	40	students	
NSITES	6	locations	
MAILXFEE	$ 3.00		overnight
TFREQ	2		per week
NINST	4		instructors
WMINI	7	weeks	per mini
NMINI	6		per year

Figure 8-5.   *Two-day instead of overnight mail*

INTERACTION MATRIX:

FROM/TO	I	A	M	S
I		$ 5.85		
A	$ 2.75		$ 3.30	
M		$ 1.25		
S			$ -	

SUMMARY:

SINGLE	WEEKLY	MINI	MINI-ALL	YEARLY
$ 13.15	$ 26.31	$ 184.15	$ 736.59	$ 4,419.52
			ORIGINAL	$ 85,059.52
			REDUCTION	94.80%

CONTROL PANEL:		units	comment
WAGE	$ 50.00		per hour
AWAGE	$ 15.00		per hour
PTIME	0.03	hours	2 minutes
DTIME	0.08	hours	5 minutes
CTIME	0.08	hours	5 minutes
MTIME	0.08	hours	5 minutes
STIME	0.08	hours	5 minutes
RTIME	0.02	hours	1 minute
WTIME	0.08	hours	5 minutes
CPAGE	$ 0.01	per page	1 penny
NPAGES	2	pages	
NSTUD	40	students	
NSITES	6	locations	
MAILXFEE	$ -		overnight
TFREQ	2		per week
NINST	4		instructors
WMINI	7	weeks	per mini
NMINI	6		per year

Figure 8-6.   *Reducing mailing fees to zero*

CHAPTER NINE

Quick Primer: Step 4, Design Treatments

Executive Summary

During diagnosis, your goal was to identify the variables in your value model that had a significant effect on the modeled activity's value. Those variables, in turn, are linked to interactions in your activity map. The final step in Web Business Engineering is for you to design online *treatments*, ways of using the Web that support these interactions online. Specifically, up to this point you've identified cost drivers in an interaction-cost model. Those cost drivers are linked to interactions in your activity map. Your final task is to find ways of placing these interactions online that reduce the effects of the cost drivers.

Objectives

After reading this chapter you should be able to:

- *Identify the interactions in your activity map that are linked to the driver variables in your value model*

- *Apply agent and media substitutions to your business activity map*

- *Design online treatments using agent and media substitutions*

- *Model treatment values*

Introduction

Remember that your ultimate goal as a Web business engineer is to develop sites or applications—Web solutions—with high value. A Web solution is said to have high value if it significantly cuts the cost of an activity or increases the benefits of that activity. To help you accomplish this goal, we first created a business activity map, which depicted the transformation and movement of materials and information between the various agents that participated in some work activity. However, the activity map showed too many ways of using the Web. We needed another tool to help trim down the possibilities, so we created a value model that quantified the value of the activity and calculated changes to that value when the underlying material, production, distribution, and storage variables were modified. By running tests on this model, we were able to identify the variables (drivers) that had the most effect on the activity's value. These variables are associated with interactions in the activity map. Our goal now is to take those interactions and design Web solutions that treat the problems or opportunities those interactions present.

Treatment consists of the following three steps:

1. Identify the affected areas of the activity map.

2. Use agent and media substitutions to design Web treatments.

3. Model the value of the treatments.

We will look at each step in the context of the EDEC case.

Case (Continued): Finding Treatments for the EDEC Mailing Assignments

Before we continue, let's review exactly what we mean by the *Web*. In the context of a Web treatment or Web solution, the *Web* is an application you develop that runs on a Web server and to which Web browsers connect. Most of the time when we refer to "designing a Web treatment," we mean the Web application that you develop. But keep in mind that in actually *implementing* your Web treatment, you may have to acquire the Web server and the computers running the browsers, particularly if those technologies aren't already available. Finally, when we use the Web as an agent in our activity maps, it is shorthand for depicting the Web server and browsers on which our application runs.

Step 1. Identify the Affected Areas of the Activity Map

In the last chapter we determined that the big value driver—a cost driver—was the Mail Express fee (MAILXFEE). Our next task is to find the interactions in the activity map that are associated with this driver. To do so, simply note the cells in the interaction matrix that contain that term. The interaction matrix shows that MAILXFEE appeared in the cost equations of two cells: A → M and R → M (see Figure 9-1; A → M depicted only):

In our activity map (see Figure 9-2), the A → M cell corresponds with the assistant sending a package of assignments (2. package: assignments) to Mail Express, and the R → M cell corresponds with the mailing room sending a package of completed assignments (6. package: completed assignments) to Mail Express.

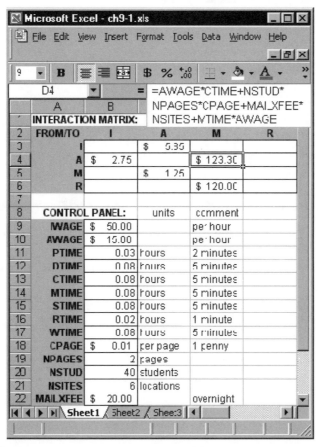

Figure 9-1. *MAILXFEE as part of the A → M cost equation.*

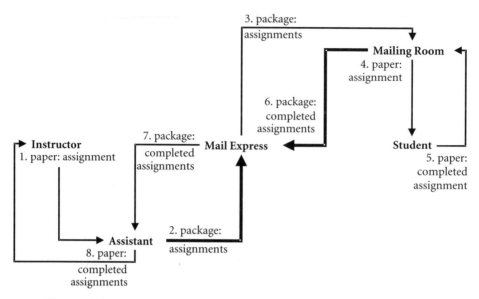

Figure 9-2.   *The interactions associated with the MAILXFEE cost driver*

Mark those areas on your map.[1] Those regions represent the affected areas of the activity map where, at the very least, you need to apply a treatment. Our final step is to design treatments for those areas.

Step 2. Use Agent and Media Substitutions to Design Web Treatments

Remember that when you design a Web treatment for some offline activity, the ultimate goal is to invent a new activity that makes use of the Web and that has higher value than the purely offline version. To accomplish this, what we want to do is take the affected areas and somehow apply the Web to them. Specifically, our interaction-cost model from the last chapter identified cost drivers, factors that drove up the cost of the assignment mailings. To design an online version of the assignment mailings that has more value than its offline counterpart, we need to decrease the effects of these cost drivers. To do so, we apply the Web to the areas of the activity map affected by the cost drivers.

---

[1]There are several ways to highlight these areas, depending on what you're using to draw your map. If you're using a drawing package, simply boldface the labels and make your connecting arrows heavy. If you are drawing them on paper or a board, you can underline the agents and materials/information.

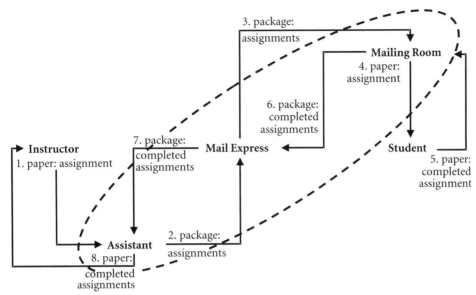

Figure 9-3. *Applying the Web to the entire affected area*

Treatment 1: Substituting Agents

The most basic way to apply the Web to the affected areas of the activity map is by substituting it for the agents or information in those regions. One possibility is to substitute the Web for *all* the affected agents (see Figure 9-3). Note that this kind of substitution replaces certain unaffected areas as well. In particular, the information areas labeled "3. package: assignments" and "7. package: complete assignments" were not marked as affected areas (see Figure 9-2); however, the agents—assistant, Mail Express, mailing room—linked to these pieces of information are affected.

Let's redraw the activity map so we can see the proposed substitution more clearly (see Figure 9-4).

Immediately we see the problem with this solution. If we substitute the Web for all the affected agents, it needs to be able to input and output content on paper. Unfortunately, as it is, the Web cannot do this. So if we indeed want to use the Web in this manner, we need to make some changes to either the agents that interact with the Web, or to the information that the agents exchange with the Web, or both. Before we do this, it is helpful to look at non-Web treatments.

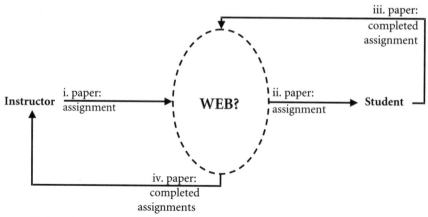

Figure 9-4. *Substituting the Web for the assistant, Mail Express, and the mailing room*

Non-Web Substitutes

As an aside, remember that the Web is only one kind of online technology. If the initial substitution of the Web is not immediately feasible, there may be other online technologies that may directly work. For example, although the Web cannot input and output paper, there is an online technology that does. Can you think of it? It may not be as "high tech" as the Web, but it will work. Give up? That online technology is a fax machine (see Figure 9-5).

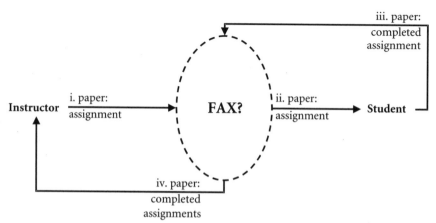

Figure 9-5. *The fax machine as a "low-tech" substitute*

This fax solution may be just as good as a Web-based one in terms of cutting the assignment mailing costs. When doing agent substitutions you need to get in the habit of looking beyond the Web to other online technologies that may apply. You may be able to come up with a solution that realizes the same benefits without using the Web, or your final solution may combine both the Web and other online technologies.

Let us assume, however, that you must use the Web. What changes are needed to make the Web work?

Treatment 2: Substituting Media

One straightforward change you can make is a media substitution. Instead of the agents exchanging paper information with the Web, they exchange the information in an electronic format that the Web can handle. The content stays the same, and the instructors and students are still dealing with assignment and completed assignments; only the medium changes (Figure 9-6).

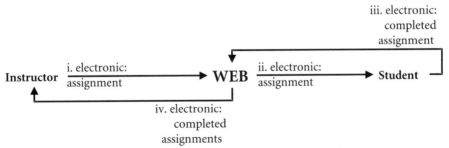

Figure 9-6. *Media substitution (Web Solution 1)*

Note, however, that this change in medium implies that both the instructor and the students assume extra "production" responsibilities—they now need to transform what was on paper into an electronic form suitable for the Web—so production costs for both agents are increased. But with most of today's software capable of saving files in the proper electronic formats, this is not an unreasonable solution.[2]

---

[2]For example, Microsoft Word™ not only can save documents as HTML files but can save them directly to a directory on a Web server. Moreover, there are many translators available that will take files in one format and convert them into an electronic format suitable for the Web, such as HTML or PDF.

Treatment 3: Adding Bridges

In those instances where an agent's activities are fixed, you have to add bridging agents. For example, instructors may not want to take on the added activity of converting their assignments into an electronic format, and they may not want to grade electronic assignments. Therefore, using the Web means that you have to add a bridge between the instructor and the Web. One solution is to hire an assistant that converts the paper assignments into an electronic version and uploads it to the Web; the students still hand in an electronic version of the assignment, but it is printed out for the instructor (see Figure 9-7).

The assistant and printer are bridging agents. They allow the instructor to perform the same assignment activities he or she has been doing all along; the bridging agents make it possible to convert the instructor's assignments into a format the Web can handle and also convert the completed assignments on the Web into a format—paper—that the instructor can more easily use.

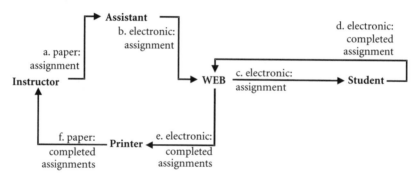

Figure 9-7.   *Adding an assistant and printer as bridging agents (Web Solution 2)*

Step 3. Model Treatment Values

The final step is to determine the value of the newly designed online activities. To do this, we first create an interaction-cost model for each solution.

Web Solution 1: Cost of the Instructor → Web Interaction

For our first Web solution (see Figure 9-6), the instructor simply finds the assignment and saves it to the Web. So the cost of the I → W interaction is the time it takes to find the assignment and save it to the Web multiplied by the instructor's wage rate:

$$I \rightarrow W: \quad IWAGE \times STIME$$

This cost combines both production and distribution costs. There are no material costs.

Web Solution 1: Cost of the Web → Instructor Interaction

Once students upload their assignments to the Web, the instructor must spend some time taking the assignments off the Web and downloading them to his or her hard drive for later grading. So the cost of the W → I interaction is this download time multiplied by the instructor's wage rate:

$$I \rightarrow W: \text{ IWAGE} \times \text{DTIME}$$

Similar to the I → W interaction, there are no material costs, and (hard drive) storage costs are assumed negligible.

Web Solution 1: Interaction-Cost Model

Let's assume that an instructor makes $50/hour and it takes 10 minutes to upload and download assignments. We can now create an interaction-cost model for our proposed Web solution (see Figure 9-8). Finally, we can determine the value of Web Solution 1 in terms of ROI. We see that Web Solution 1 results in a cost reduction of over 90%!

Web Solution 1: ROI

Each year Web Solution 1 saves EDEC $79,459.52; $5,600 per year for Web-based assignment distribution versus $85,059.52 per year for distributing assignments via Mail Express. Let's assume that to implement this solution EDEC must spend $20,000 on a Web server and $10,000 for your consultation and development fees. We can now calculate the value of Web Solution 1 (see Figure 9-9; also refer to Chapter 4 for an explanation). Over three years, Web Solution 1 gives EDEC an

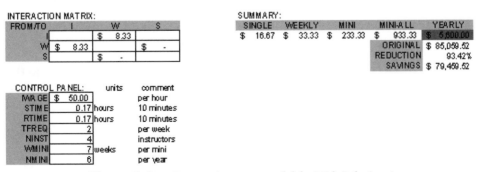

Figure 9-8. *Interaction-cost model for Web Solution 1*

	YEAR 0	YEAR 1	YEAR 2	YEAR 3
BENEFITS	0	$ 79,459.52	$ 79,459.52	$ 79,459.52
COSTS	$ 30,000.00	$ -	$ -	$ -
PROFITS	$ (30,000.00)	$ 79,459.52	$ 79,459.52	$ 79,459.52
CASH FLOW	$ (30,000.00)	$69,095.23	$60,082.81	$52,245.92
NPV		$ 39,095.23	$ 99,178.05	$ 151,423.97
ROI		130%	331%	505%

Figure 9-9.   *The value of Web Solution 1 over several years.*
(15% discount rate used for NPV calculations)

ROI of 505%, with a first-year ROI of 130%![3] Remember that most managers accept projects with an ROI of 20%. Next, let's take a look at our Web solution with bridges.

Web Solution 2: Cost of the Instructor → Assistant Interaction

In our second Web solution (see Figure 9-7), the instructor gives a paper version of the assignment to an assistant who converts the assignment into an electronic format suitable for distribution over the Web. The students complete the assignments and upload them to the Web. Finally, the Web automatically prints out the students' completed assignments onto a printer inside of the instructor's office. EDEC only has control over instructor-assistant, assistant-Web, and printer-instructor interaction costs.

The production cost of the I → A interaction is a function of the time it takes to find and print the document (PTIME) multiplied by the instructor's wage rate (IWAGE). The material cost is the number of pages in the assignment (NPAGES) multiplied by the cost of a page (CPAGE). The distribution cost is the time it takes the instructor to walk the assignment over to the assistant (DTIME) multiplied by the instructor's wage rate (IWAGE). Altogether, the cost of the I → A interaction is:

$$\mathbf{I \rightarrow A:} \quad IWAGE \times PTIME + NPAGES \times CPAGE + IWAGE \times DTIME$$

Web Solution 2: Cost of the Assistant → Web Interaction

The production cost of the A → W interaction is the time it takes to convert the paper assignment into an electronic format (CTIME) multiplied by the assistant's

---

[3]Remember we defined ROI is profits/cost. To calculate the ROI for a given year, add the present value (PV) of the benefits up to that year, and divide by the initial (year 0) costs. For example, the year 2 ROI is: $\frac{60,082.81 + 69,095.23 - 30,000}{30,000} = 3.31 = 331\%$ (*Note:* For the purposes of instruction we are ignoring the factors of taxes and depreciation; assume a 15% discount rate for NPV calculations.)

wage rate (AWAGE). The distribution cost is the time it takes to upload the converted assignment onto the Web (MTIME) multiplied by the assistant's wage rate (AWAGE). There are no material costs, so the cost of the A → W interaction is:

> **A → W:** AWAGE × CTIME + AWAGE × MTIME

Web Solution 2: Cost of the Printer → Instructor Interaction

Because the Web automatically prints the completed assignment onto a printer in the instructor's office, the only cost is a material cost. In particular, the material cost is the number of pages in the completed assignment (NPAGES—we will assume it's the same number of pages as the assignment) multiplied by the number of students turning in assignments (NSTUD) multiplied by the cost of a page (CPAGE). The cost of the P → I interaction is:

> **P → I:** NPAGES × NSTUD × CPAGE

Web Solution 2: Interaction-Cost Model

Let's assume that the instructor makes $50/hour (IWAGE), the assistant makes $15/hour (AWAGE), conversion time takes 30 minutes (CTIME), upload time takes 10 minutes (MTIME), and all other values are similar to those in the interaction-cost model for the offline mailing activity. We can construct an interaction-cost model as shown in Figure 9-10.

Note that the savings for Web Solution 2 is almost exactly the same as the first solution. To determine which one to recommend, we need to look at the value of Web Solution 2, terms of ROI.

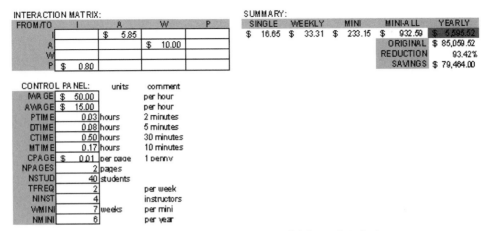

Figure 9-10. *Interaction-cost model for Web Solution 2*

Web Solution 2: ROI

Web Solution 2's savings may be similar to Web Solution 1's, but the initial and ongoing costs for Web Solution 2 are different. Similar to Web Solution 1, EDEC must buy a Web server for $20,000 and pay you a consulting and development fee of $10,000. However, there are training costs as well. The assistant has to be trained to convert files into, say, HTML. Let's assume the assistant takes a one-week HTML training course that costs $1,000. There is also the cost of the printers that go into the instructors' offices, which we will set at $2,000. Finally, for the sake of illustration, let's assume that EDEC buys a yearly maintenance contract for the printers at $500 per year. We calculate the value of treatment 2 as shown in Figure 9-11.

We see that Web Solution 2 has a lower ROI than Web Solution 1 across all three years. Thus, although Web Solution 2 has a slightly higher savings than Web Solution 1, its overall value is less due to the higher initial costs ($33K versus $30K) and the ongoing maintenance costs ($500). Thus, Web Solution 1 is the solution with the highest value and the one we recommend to EDEC.

This concludes my quick primer on Web Business Engineering. If you've made it this far—congratulations! You are on your way to developing high-value business Web sites. My primary goal was to present just enough of the key concepts so that you could immediately start applying Web Business Engineering to your own situations. To this end I chose an example from my own experience that was concise yet complex enough to clearly illustrate the key ideas in each of the steps. However, Web Business Engineering has a much broader application than what I've shown in this chapter. Next, we will see Web Business Engineering used in a variety of different applications that are relevant to both Web consultants and Web entrepreneurs.

	YEAR 0	YEAR 1	YEAR 2	YEAR 3
BENEFITS	0	$ 79,464.00	$ 79,464.00	$ 79,464.00
COSTS	$ 33,000.00	$ 500.00	$ 500.00	$ 500.00
PROFITS	$ (33,000.00)	$ 78,964.00	$ 78,964.00	$ 78,964.00
CASH FLOW	$ (33,000.00)	$68,664.35	$59,708.13	$51,920.11
NPV		$ 35,664.35	$ 95,372.48	$ 147,292.59
ROI		108%	289%	446%

Figure 9-11. *The value of treatment 1 over several years (15% discount rate used for NPV calculations)*

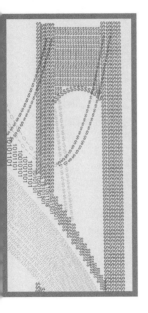

Case Studies: Putting Offline Activities Online

In the previous section I provided a quick overview of the key concepts in Web Business Engineering (WBE) and demonstrated their application on an actual business activity. This section presents a demonstration of the flexibility of WBE. It is used to solve four different kinds of problems: a small business, a large institution, a social, and an online marketing problem. Chapter 10 presents innovative ways of using the Web to support the activities of a small business that, on the surface, does not appear suitable for the Web. Chapter 11 applies WBE to a large institution's internal processes, using it to discover a cost-effective way of using the Web to support an online version of a paper-based procedure. Chapter 12 shows how to find dates on the Web. Finally, demonstrating that WBE is not just for discovering how to support offline activities online, Chapter 13 shows the use of WBE to analyze online activities and discover new ways to drive traffic to a Web site.

CHAPTER TEN

WBE in Small Businesses: The Case of the Hair Salon

Executive Summary

To illustrate the power of Web Business Engineering, let's apply it to a business that has no apparent use for the Web beyond advertising. The business's managers are "early adopters." Their primary goal is to find innovative ways of using the Web instead of using it to generate more revenues or cut costs. Web Business Engineering can help discover innovative Web content that has the added benefit of being aligned with existing business processes. We contrast Web Business Engineering with the "electronic paper" approach to determining Web content. In the latter, a site's content is driven by the concept that the Web is a kind of electronic paper; if you have an idea for content that can be put on paper, then it's also appropriate Web content. However, unlike Web Business Engineering, the electronic paper approach—which is not based on a business's processes—can actually lead to content that is contrary to a business's existing practices.

Objectives

After reading this chapter you should be able to:

■ *Create multiple maps of different activities in the same business*

■ *Apply Web Business Engineering to find innovative ways of using the Web in a small business that go beyond the uses of the "Web as electronic paper"*

■ *Explain how using Web Business Engineering leads to solutions that are aligned with a business's existing practices*

■ *Use analogies between offline activities to discover additional Web treatments*

Introduction

Perhaps the ultimate test of any new Web design technique, such as Web Business Engineering (WBE), is its successful application to a seemingly "impossible" business situation, a situation where the Web doesn't seem applicable at all. With this in mind, we'll begin with a business that on the surface doesn't appear to have any business being on the Web: a hair salon. While computers are capable of many wonderful things, I think most of us will agree that cutting hair isn't one of them. As such, the Web—as a computing technology—doesn't appear to be a valuable tool for a hair salon beyond its obvious use for electronic advertising.

Some readers are probably taking exception to the statement that a hair salon has limited Web uses. Students often comment that if *they* had to put a hair salon on the Web, they would add content like pictures of different hairstyles, an online ordering system for hair care products such as shampoos and conditioners, and making online appointments. These ideas *are* valid ways for a hair salon to use the Web, but because they are based on a view of the Web that is not grounded in a business's existing practices—the Web as electronic paper/catalog—they may conflict with those practices.

By systematically applying WBE, we should be able to find innovative ways of using the Web that go beyond this view of the Web as a kind of electronic paper and that have the added benefit of being aligned with existing business practices. So we will examine how WBE *can* find innovative ways of using the Web for a hair salon that conform to the salon's existing practices. We will also see how the conventional view of the Web as electronic paper leads to Web content that either supports only a small part of the salon's overall practices or conflicts with existing practices.

Case Study: Hair Crafters

Hair Crafters' management team approached me in early 1994, when the Web was still in its infancy. Interviews with the Hair Crafters management team revealed that they fit into the category of "early technology adopters." While they ultimately wanted to use the Web to make money, their primary goal in establishing a Web site was to get a sense of what the technology could offer them beyond an electronic catalog/advertisement. They wanted a Web site that was different from anything currently out there.

Given management's requests, the problem facing the Web Business Engineer is one of innovation. For these types of problems, the goal is to find a use of the Web that is aligned with existing high-value, offline business practices, not necessarily just to save costs or generate revenues. To solve this problem, let's first take a look at a typical day at Hair Crafters.

Typical Operation

The customer (henceforth, C) arrives the day of the appointment and checks in at the reception desk. If this is C's first visit, the receptionist (R) asks C to fill out a two-page, new-client form, which includes blanks for name, address, and hair problems, along with marketing questions, such as why the customer chose Hair Crafters. The majority of customers have scheduled their appointments ahead of time. When they get to the salon, they tell the receptionist their name and appointment time. After verifying the appointment, R tells C to have a seat in the waiting area until the stylist (S) is ready for C. When called, C sits in a chair and first discusses with S the kind of haircut he or she wants. S then shampoos C's hair and returns C to the chair and cuts his or her hair. S and C go to the reception desk, where S suggests hair care products to C. C then pays for the haircut and hair care products, and the receptionist makes a future appointment for C (see Figure 10-1).

Products

To understand the information and information practices that support the business, we must identify the products of the business. A product is operationalized as anything the customer leaves the business with that he or she did not have upon entering. This includes any knowledge the customer acquires as a consequence of interacting with employees, tools, or other artifacts within the business. The business sees its products as the haircut and hair care products. Repeated observations of what a customer takes away from the business will usually reveal all other products except for knowledge products.

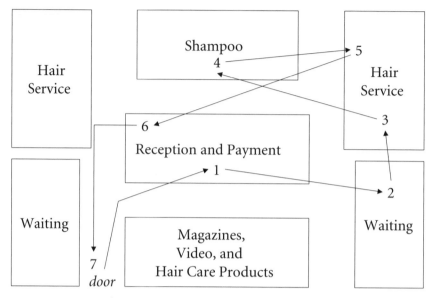

Figure 10-1.   *Hair Crafters salon layout*

Observing a customer's arrival and departure suggests four products:

1. Hair service

2. A reminder card for a return visit

3. Hair care products

4. A payment receipt for services and/or products

I'll focus on analyzing the information activities surrounding the first three products, as the last one gets into online payment issues, which is a subject that has been thoroughly researched.

Step 1: Map Business Activity (Haircut)

We'll continue to assume that the service performed was a haircut. The key information activity for a haircut comes right before the hair is actually cut, where the customer and stylist discuss what kind of haircut the customer wants. Part of the difficulty in mapping the haircut activity is that the medium holding the content is not readily apparent; the stylist and customer communicate much of their information either verbally or visually instead of on paper or electronically. Thus, the hair salon provides a good case for applying Web Business Engineering techniques on nonconventional media. A lot of the initial confusion when applying business engineering techniques centers around what qualifies as an information medium (remember, a medium is anything that holds content). Therefore, in this discussion of the haircutting activity, whenever an information medium—or an activity involving an information medium—is mentioned, the medium's abbreviation is placed in parentheses. This abbreviation—a lowercased letter—is also used in the business activity map.

The haircut activity is actually divided into two parts, style specification and detail specification.

Style Specification

Style specification is the activity when the customer gives the stylist a rough idea of what kind of haircut he or she wants. Four situations were observed:

1. The customer (C) had a style in mind and told (a) the stylist (S) about it.

2. The customer (C) saw a style he or she liked in a magazine and brought a picture (P) of it to show (v) the stylist (S).

3. The customer did not know what style he or she wanted and had the stylist recommend (a) one.

4. The customer told (a) the stylist to cut it similar to the previous haircut.

However, it is not as simple as telling the stylist what kind of haircut the customer wants, as the style may not be appropriate for the type of hair the customer has. The stylist needs to examine how the customer's hair grows, the texture of the hair, and other factors to determine the suitability of a particular style. Note that in doing so the stylist uses several different information modalities, both visual (v) and tactile (t). If a style does not fit the customer's hair type, then both stylist and customer must negotiate (a) a compromise.

Detail Specification

Once the stylist understands what kind of haircut the customer wants, they discuss (a) specific haircut details, such as length. In these discussions, the mirror (M) plays an important role in helping the customer and stylist arrive at a common understanding of what needs to be done. For example, a stylist is often observed sliding parts of the customer's hair between his or her fingers and asking the customer the appropriate length to cut. These discussions occur while both customer and stylist are looking at the customer's reflection in the mirror. The information activity for a haircut can be mapped as shown in Figure 10-2.

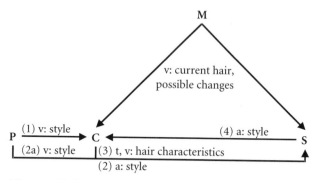

Figure 10-2.   *Map of the haircut specification activity*

Step 1: Map Business Activity (Hair Care Products)

Given the many information activities that take place in a hair salon, how does the business engineer know which ones are specific to a given product? Part of the answer can be found by looking at the information that precedes or occurs during the design or construction of a product. For example, for the haircut (product) the discussions (information activity) that occurred prior to and during the haircut were specific to the haircut.

However, there are products where the important information activity occurs way before the product is created. The hair care products are typically this. The information activity that occurs when the customer buys the product is not as important as the information activity that makes the customer buy the product in the first place. But to map this activity we need to know where it is. This brings us back to the question posed at the beginning of this section: How does the business engineer know which information activities are specific to a given product?

The answer is that information activity belongs to a product if that activity contains information that pertains to the product. To discover the key information activity for the hair care product, the Web business engineer needs to examine the activity surrounding the customer as he or she visits the various stations in the salon (see Figure 10-1), looking for information that is related to hair care products. In doing so one finds that while washing the customer's hair, the stylist typically (a) asks the customer if he or she has any problems with his or her hair.

If the customer says (a) "yes", the stylist then tells (a) the customer about specific Hair Crafters hair care products that can solve those problems. This kind of dialog also occurs while the stylist cuts the customer's hair. This kind of activity can be mapped as shown in Figure 10-3.

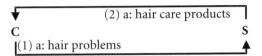

Figure 10-3. *Map of hair care product discussions*

Step 1: Map Business Activity (Reminder Card)

The final activity to map is the information activity surrounding the reminder card. Prior to leaving the salon, the customer, accompanied by the stylist, stops at the reception table to pay for the haircut and any hair care products. At this time, the receptionist asks the customer if he or she would like to schedule a return visit. The customer (C) then gives (a) the stylist (S) and receptionist (R) a desired return date. R looks (v) at the appointment book (b) and gives (a) C a list of open days and times. C picks one (a), S writes (m) the date and time on the reminder card (M), and S gives the card to C. The day before the appointment, R telephones (p) C with a reminder. Figure 10-4 shows the map for this activity.

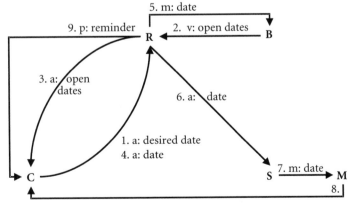

Figure 10-4. *Map for the reminder card*

Steps 2 and 3: Model Activity Value, Diagnose Problems and Opportunities

Because Hair Crafters' business managers are interested in discovering innovative ways of using the Web for their business and not to cut costs or generate revenues, we can skip the modeling and diagnosis steps. Instead, let's go straight to the information activity map to discover online treatments. Agent substitutions are combined with medium substitutions to discover ways of using the Web to support key activities in Hair Crafters.

Step 4: Design Treatments

Hair Care Product Discussions

Let's start with the discussion surrounding the hair care products. Much of this discussion is verbal. The customer relates his or her hair care problems, and the stylist tells the customer about products that solve those problems. Drawing our process bubble around the stylist shows that if the Web is to replace the stylist, it must be capable of getting hair problems and returning hair care products (see Figure 10-5).

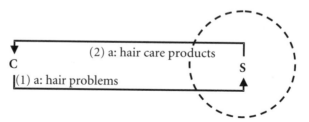

Figure 10-5. *The stylist as a potential Web substitute*

To accomplish this requires a simple change of medium. Instead of the hair problems delivered verbally, the customer can type in his or her hair care problems. Then, instead of the product recommendations being made verbally, the Web site can display which hair care products are needed (see Figure 10-6).

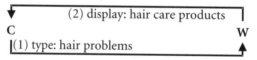

Figure 10-6. *Using the Web to recommend products*

The benefits of a Web "product expert" over a simple electronic catalog are clear. With an electronic catalog, customers must read product descriptions and decide for themselves which products best meet their needs. With a product expert, customers enter their problems, and the decision of what to buy is automatically made for them (see Figure 10-7).

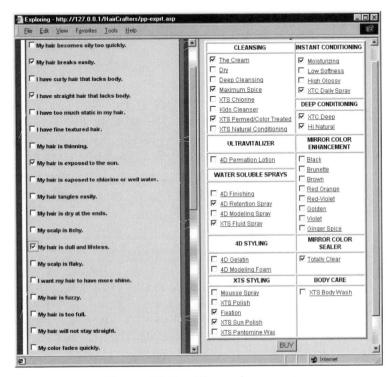

Figure 10-7. *The product expert*

At this point, we can see how the Web, while supporting existing work practices, also introduces new work practices into the salon. For example, the same technology that is used to help customers decide which hair care products solve their particular hair problems can be used by stylists in training to help them learn which products solve which problems (see Figure 10-8).

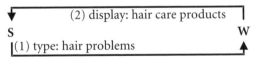

Figure 10-8. *Web as instructional tool*

Stuff That Can't Be Put Online: The Haircut

In the best case, putting the haircut recommendation online translates into substituting the Web for all the agents in the haircut recommendation (Figure 10-9).

Using the Web to substitute for haircut pictures is straightforward. Instead of looking at pictures in a magazine, the customer looks at a computer screen. Steps 2, 3, and 4 involve recommending a style to a customer. Steps 2 and 4 involve media (a) that the Web can easily substitute for; information exchanged verbally can be changed to communication via a keyboard and computer screen.

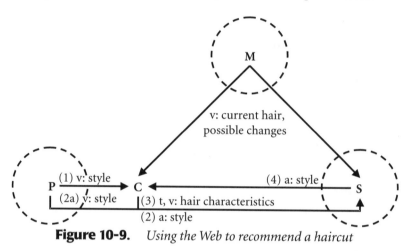

Figure 10-9.   *Using the Web to recommend a haircut*

It would appear that putting the haircut recommendation activity online is a straightforward matter: Get a picture of the customer, have a database of pictures of different hairstyles, and then superimpose the different hairstyles onto the customer's picture. But reality is not that simple. Part of the activity of recommending a style to the customer requires that the stylist examine the customer's hair characteristics (thickness, growth patterns) to see if the desired hairstyle fits the customer's hair type. This information is communicated to the stylist by looking at and touching the customer's hair. If the haircut recommendation activity is to be put online, then the customer needs some way of unambiguously communicating his or her hair characteristics to the Web. Unfortunately, current technology does not allow this kind of information to be easily communicated. Thus, the haircut recommendation activity is not a good candidate for online handling.

Finally, the haircut cannot be put online—at least not yet—because it is physical, not informational activity. So, our use of the Web is limited to providing pictures of different hairstyles that can possibly be printed out and shown to the stylist (see Figure 10-10).

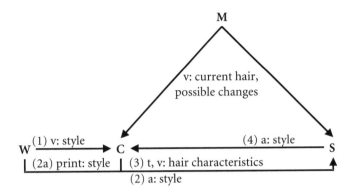

Figure 10-10. *The Web as a minimal part of the haircut activity*

Reminder Card

Although a reminder card is not your typical product, the information activities and information products surrounding the reminder card can be usefully handled online. The entire activity of scheduling a haircut appointment offline (Steps 1 to 6) can be easily made an online scheduling activity. More important, the entire reminding activity (Steps 7 to 9) can be placed online. The paper reminder card can be replaced by an electronic reminder, which can be sent (via e-mail) the day before the haircut, instead of being phoned in.

Other Web Uses: The Importance of Analogy

During Web Business Engineering, one often discovers ways of using the Web that can apply to situations beyond the offline situation from which they were originally derived. Take the reminder activity; the reminder is originally intended just for the haircut appointments, but there is no reason why the reminding activity cannot extend to other services as well, like the hair care products.

The reason reminders are done only for haircut appointments is because it is probably easy for both the stylist and the customer to estimate when the customer will need another haircut. However, it is not as easy to estimate when a customer will need another bottle of hair conditioner or shampoo. Thus, reminding is done offline only for the haircut. Moving activities online inherits many of the benefits of the online technology, such as the ability of the technology to keep records of user activity and calculate statistics. For example, instead of the customer estimating how long it will take to use up a bottle of shampoo, the customer can simply buy shampoo off the Web site. After a number of such purchases, the Web site can estimate when the customer is likely to buy a new bottle of shampoo, and it can send off a reminder (see Figure 10-11).

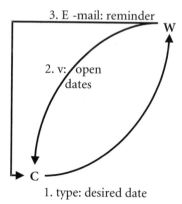

Figure 10-11. *Putting the reminder card online*

Table 10-1 summarizes the Web content suggested by the catalog metaphor versus the content suggested by the Web Business Engineering approach. Although certain content is common to both approaches, the Web Business Engineering approach is more closely aligned with existing business activities.

Table 10-1. Catalog versus Web Business Engineering

Products	Electronic Paper/ Catalog Approach	Web Business Engineering
Haircut	Picture and description of styles of haircuts performed Haircut prices	Mechanism for determining the suitability of a customer's hair to his or her desired hairstyle
Hair Care Products	Pictures and descriptions of hair care products Prices Mechanism for online purchasing	Mechanism for determining which products solve the customer's hair problems
Reminder Card	N/A (not a product under the catalog approach)	E-mail reminders Online appointments

CHAPTER ELEVEN

WBE in Large Institutions: The Online Survey Case

Executive Summary

Most businesses first use the Web as a substitute for paper-based procedures: Activities that use paper become activities that use the Web. The goal is to totally eliminate any paper used in the old procedure and handle all information gathering, processing, and distribution online. But is it really necessary for one to implement a completely online solution? Can a *partially* paperless implementation still provide significant benefits? Without Web Business Engineering it is difficult to answer these questions, and the safest approach is to put the entire activity online. However, this can be expensive in terms of both time and cost. In this chapter we examine one such paper-based procedure—student course evaluations at the department of a large university—with the goal of determining the extent to which paper should be eliminated. Those portions of the activity that are candidates for online handling are identified. We will see that it is possible to achieve order of magnitude benefits without putting the entire course survey procedure on the Web. Thus, to avoid overkill, high development costs, and/or wasted time, one should use Web Business Engineering before placing any paper-based procedure online.

Objectives

After reading this chapter you should be able to:

■ *Correctly place an offline paper-based procedure online*

■ *Annotate business activity maps with cardinality*

Introduction

One of the most common uses of the Web is as a substitute for paper-based activities. For example, most businesses first think of using the Web as an advertising tool, electronic catalog, or electronic brochure. These are all examples of applications with paper-based counterparts such as paper advertising, mail-order catalogs, and paper brochures. Although it is frequently done, it is unwise for a business to blindly place anything that is on paper onto the Web. If one can demonstrate high value in using the Web as a substitute for paper, then it is appropriate. Unfortunately, more often than not, businesses don't have a systematic, *value-based* plan for moving a paper-based procedure online. Then one of two things happens: Either the online procedure is indeed better or it isn't. Unfortunately, the latter is usually the case. Some aspects of the new, online procedure are better and some aren't, which makes for an overall less efficient procedure. Take, for example, a paper-based procedure like grading reports. Suppose an instructor decides that all students should turn in electronic copies of reports. What usually happens is that both homework submissions and returning graded reports are more efficient (faster), but the actual grading takes longer because it's more difficult to mark up an electronic report. Thus, the paperless, online activity—all things considered—is less efficient than the paper-based version. Ideally, you want to put online only those aspects of a procedure that add high value, but this is easier said than done.

In this chapter we examine how you use Web Business Engineering to determine the best way to handle an offline paper-based activity online. The specific activity we will work with is the student course evaluations at a department in a large university. First, WBE information activity maps are used to identify those portions of the activity that are likely candidates for online handling. To aid us in doing so, I introduce a new annotation for the activitiy maps: cardinality. Cardinality depicts the "how many" relationship between the agents that participate in an information transaction. Cardinality values include one to one, one to many, many to one, and many to many. By annotating the map with cardinality, the Web business engineer gets a quick idea of where revenues or costs can be magnified, and these areas constitute likely candidates for online handling. We also explore how to use WBE value models to determine which aspects of an activity are worth putting online. We will see that order of magnitude benefits can be accomplished without having to implement a completely paperless survey.

Case Study: Background

The Department of Computational Ecology (DCE) is one of the top computational ecology programs in the country, boasting an annual class size of 700 students. Ironically, the technology used in the program lags behind this top ranking. Many routine student activities, such as registering for classes, checking course descriptions, and checking grades, are either paper-based or conducted on information systems with clumsy text-based user interfaces. Informal student surveys indicate a high level of dissatisfaction with DCE's use of technology in the program. Thus, the department Chair, hereafter "the Chair," has made the creation of a Web-based student information system a top priority.

The Chair, however, would like to take an inside-out approach. Recognizing that peripheral activities (student activities) cannot be made efficient through technology without central activities (administrative activities) being technologically efficient, the Chair requests some use of the Web that improves administrative functions. Furthermore, in order to justify the high cost associated with future Web-based systems development, the Chair needs a solution that has an immediate and quantifiable impact.

On the surface, this problem appears to be one of innovation. However, there are numerous constraints on this problem that make it more than simply an innovation problem. The Chair wants a Web-based solution but does not know exactly what that system should be. Thus, the main job of the Web business engineer is to come up with such a system. However, the constraint that the Web solution has an immediate and quantifiable impact means that the problem is either one of generating revenues or cutting costs. Now, had the Chair asked for a Web-based solution for peripheral activities, such as recruiting new students or better ties with alumni, then a revenue-generating solution would be appropriate. However, the final constraint that the information system be used to improve central, administrative activities suggests that the problem is one of cutting costs.

Overview of the Course Evaluation Survey

When cutting costs, the easiest way to use the Web is as a substitute for another information medium, like paper. One particularly paper-intensive procedure was the course evaluation survey. DCE was on the minisemester system instead of the semester system (two minisemesters were the equivalent of one semester). There were six minisemesters in a year, which includes two summer sessions. At the end of each minisemester, students were given a 22-question survey, which covered the quality of the materials and instruction, among other course-related issues. There were approximately 64 courses taught each minisemester. Each course had on average 40 students, which translated into approximately 2,500 paper surveys each minisemester—assuming all students filled out all surveys. Typically, however, only 60 percent of the students filled out the paper surveys. The 60 percent response rate provided a good milestone for a Web-based course survey system.

Typical Operation

Early in the course survey activity, an administrative assistant is in charge of printing out the survey questions for each class. Each class gets the same set of survey questions; the only difference is that the instructor's name, the course, and section number are printed on the top of the survey for later sorting. The assistant gets one student from each class to serve as a "gopher." The gopher is responsible for going to class, distributing surveys, and collecting surveys. Gophers are assigned haphazardly. The assistant (1) flags down students as they pass by her office, (2) asks them what class they are in, and (3) asks if they would like to distribute surveys to their class. If a student agrees, the assistant gives the student a manila folder with the appropriate surveys.

The gophers distribute the surveys during the first 5 minutes of class. The students are given 10 minutes to finish the survey. The gophers then spend an additional 5 minutes collecting surveys. In all, approximately 20 minutes of lecture time is lost to filling out surveys per course. After class, the gophers return the surveys to the administrative assistant.

Once the administrative assistant gets all the surveys, she reenters the information into a computer. Eighteen of the questions are five-part multiple-choice questions. The remaining four questions are free-form responses. The computer program creates a number of summaries.

1. An overall summary that displays the course number, the instructor, and the answers to questions 17 and 18 (question 17 asks the students if they would recommend the course, and question 18 asks if they would recommend

the instructor), along with how many students filled out the survey and the class size.

2. An individual instructor summary, which displays the average of each question for the course taught.

3. The average of each question across all courses.

The survey procedure does not end with the computer summaries. The assistant staples a copy of the summary they typed for questions 19 through 22 (the free-form comments) to the individual instructor summary (2). They also summarize the percentage of students that completed the survey. Finally, the Chair gets a copy of the computer summaries. If an instructor scored particularly well, the Chair sends a letter of congratulations to that instructor.

Products

Although on the surface it seems as if there is only one product—survey results— the survey results are actually three different products: one for students, one for the faculty that taught, and one for the Chair.

1. *Survey results (student version).* The student's version of the survey displays all the courses taught for the minisemester, who taught what course, and the average of questions 17 and 18 ("Would you recommend this course to other students?" and "Would you recommend this instructor?").

2. *Survey results (faculty version).* Each faculty member gets a copy of the entire 22-question survey, which consists of the average for each multiple-choice question (questions 1–18) and a summary of the text for the free-form questions (questions 19–22).

3. *Survey results (Chair version).* The department chair of the school gets a summary of the survey, which includes summaries 1 and 2 above, and a summary of the average of each question across all courses. The Chair uses this information for a number of later decisions, such as pay raises or whether an instructor will teach the same course next year.

Several items may contain information from the course survey activity but are not actually part of it. For example, the congratulations letter that the Chair sends to faculty with high course ratings contains information from the course survey, but it is actually part of a different activity—pay and promotions. We can now map the activity surrounding each of the different products.

Step 1: Map Activity (Distributing the Survey)

The map starts with the survey collection and distribution activity. First, the administrative assistant gives a folder of paper surveys to a gopher. Ideally there are 64 gophers, one for each class taught that semester. Next, each gopher then goes to class and distributes the survey to the students in that class. The students complete the survey and return it to the gopher. The gophers then return the surveys to the assistant in a folder. There are three agents involved in this activity: the assistant (A), the gophers (G), and the students (S). One way to map this activity is as shown in Figure 11-1.

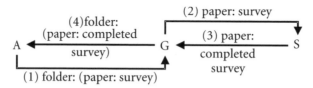

Figure 11-1.   *Survey collection activity, without annotations*

This map accurately depicts the movement of information (the surveys), but details such as how many surveys are distributed or how many agents participate in the distribution are not depicted. Specifically, there are 64 classes taught in a minisemester, so there are 64 gophers. How do the 64 gophers get represented on the same map? Furthermore, there is not just one but several surveys in the folder, one for each student in the class. On average there are 45 students per class and therefore 45 surveys per folder. How does this "how many" or *cardinality* information get depicted on the map?

Formally, there are several kinds of cardinality that must be depicted. Two are informational cardinality, which depicts one or more pieces of information, and interactional cardinality, which depicts how many of one kind of agent interacts with another kind of agent. The situation where one folder contains several surveys is an example of the need to depict informational cardinality. One administrative assistant delivering folders to (interacting with) multiple gophers is an example of the need to depict interactional cardinality.

In the figures, an asterisk is used to depict informational cardinality, specifically a "*" after a piece of information denotes zero or more instances of that information. Instead of an asterisk, you can use a plus sign or the actual number of times that information appears. To depict agent cardinality, a number or variable is placed at the base and tip of the arrows in the map. The numbers depict how many of one agent interact with another. In our example, one administrative assistant (A) gives out survey folders to 64 gophers (G), so the arrow going from A to G would have 1 at the base and 64 at its tip. To be more general, instead of 64, a variable such as "N" is typically used to denote that one-A interacts with many-G's, since what is important is that there is a one-to-many relationship and not necessarily the exact number of interactions. However, the exact numbers *will* be used in the value model as we will see later in this chapter. Figure 11-2 below depicts both informational cardinality and interactional cardinality. Let's map out the remaining subactivities using the annotation techniques described here.

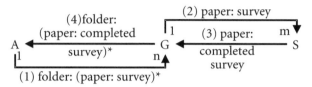

Figure 11-2.   *The survey collection activity, with annotations for informational and interactional cardinality*

Step 1: Map Activity (Result Generation)

With the folders collected, the administrative assistant (A) manually reenters each of the surveys into a computer (C). Once the information is entered, several computer programs are run that generate three different summaries of the data: one for the students to see, one for the faculty that taught, and one for the Chair. The summaries are printed out on paper (P). The assistant then takes these print-outs and makes several copies (on a copy machine, X) for distribution. This subactivity is mapped in Figure 11-3.

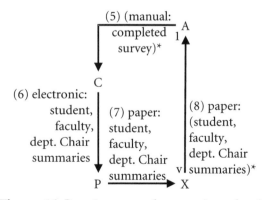

Figure 11-3.   *Survey result generation subactivity*

Step 1: Map Activity (Result Distribution)

The final part of the course survey activity is the distribution of the results. To distribute the survey results, the assistant (A) simply takes the paper summaries and hand delivers them to the department Chair (D), faculty members (F), and to the students' mailboxes (see Figure 11-4). For the sake of brevity, students' mailboxes are omitted from the map. Generally, when an agent simply relays the information to another agent, as a mailbox would do, and does not perform any transformations on the information, it is not depicted in the map. So why is the assistant (A) depicted in the map below when all she does is distribute copies? The answer is that the assistant *is* doing a transformation when she takes the copies and separates them into three different piles (one for the Chair, faculty, and students).

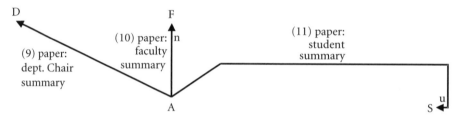

Figure 11-4.   *Survey results distribution subactivity*

We can now depict the entire map as in Figure 11-5. With our map created, we can now develop a value model of it.

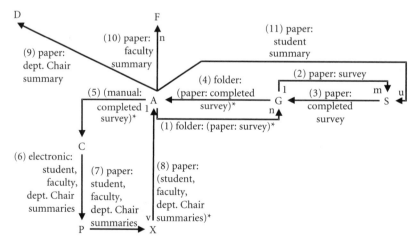

Figure 11-5.   *Entire course survey map*

Step 2: Model the Value of the Survey Activity

A → G Cost

In this interaction, the assistant makes the surveys and gives them to student gophers. There are two material costs. First is the cost of the folder (Cfolder) for each class (n) : Cfolder × n. Second is the cost of the paper that the survey is printed on (Cpaper) for all students in all courses (n × m): Cpaper × n × m. The production cost is a function of the time it takes the assistant to copy and package the surveys (Tcopysurveys and Tpackagesurveys, respectively) multiplied by the assistant's wage rate (Wa): Wa × (Tcopysurveys + Tpackagesurveys). The distribution costs are simply the time it takes to find and hand off the surveys to the gopher (Tgetgophers) multiplied by the assistant's wage rate: Wa × Tgetgophers. Altogether:

> **A→G:** Cfolder × n + Cpaper × n × m + Wa ×
> (Tcopysurveys + Tpackagesurveys + Tgetgophers)

G → S Cost

After getting the survey packet, the gopher distributes the surveys to the students (m) in his or her class. Gophers volunteer their time, so this distribution cost is zero. However, if the gopher was paid, then the cost would be the gopher's wage rate (Wg) multiplied by the time it took the gopher to distribute the surveys to the students in a given course (Tdistributesurveys). Although the gopher's wage rate is zero, it is useful to include this cost in the model because it makes it easy to simulate the scenario where DCE hires a gopher. Finally, there is a hidden cost in this interaction: the opportunity cost of filling out these surveys (Copportunity × Tdistributesurveys); the time the students spend filling out the surveys could be spent learning material. Both the distribution and opportunity costs need to be accounted for across all courses (n):

> **G→S:** (Wg × Tdistributesurveys + Copportunity × Tdistributesurveys) × n

S → G Cost

After the students finish filling out the surveys, the gopher collects them. The equation for this cost is similar to the preceding one, except that time is spent collecting versus distributing surveys (Tcollectsurveys):

> **S→G:** (Wg × Tcollectsurveys + Copportunity × Tcollectsurveys) × n

G → A Cost

The gophers return the completed surveys to the assistant. This is a distribution cost, and, because gophers volunteer their time, the cost is zero. However, for the reasons mentioned we will calculate and include the cost in our model. The cost is simply the time it takes all gophers (n) to return the surveys to the assistant (Treturnsurveys) multiplied by the gophers' wage rate (Wg):

$$\textbf{G} \rightarrow \textbf{A: } Wg \times Treturnsurveys \times n$$

A → C Cost

With the completed surveys in hand, the assistant takes each survey (n × m, in all) and enters the answers into a computer. The cost of this interaction is the time it takes to enter all the surveys (n × m × Tentersurvey) multiplied by the assistant's wage rate (Wa). This cost combines production and distribution:

$$\textbf{A} \rightarrow \textbf{C: } n \times m \times Tentersurvey \times Wa$$

C → P Cost

After the assistant keys in all the survey data, the computer prints out two summaries: (1) a detailed summary for each instructor (n in all), which is specific to the course taught, and (2) a general summary for the students, which only shows certain statistics. These costs are material costs and are a function of the cost of paper (Cpaper) multiplied by the average size of the instructor's report (avgReportSize) and the student's summary report (avgSummarySize):

$$\textbf{C} \rightarrow \textbf{P: } C\ paper \times avgReportSize \times n + Cpaper \times avgSummarySize$$

P → X Cost

The assistant makes copies of the summaries.[1] Two copies of the faculty report are made, one to be distributed to faculty and one for the department Chair. The student report is copied for all students. The costs are all material:

$$\textbf{P} \rightarrow \textbf{X: } avgReportSize \times n \times Cpaper \times 2 + avgSummarySize \times n \times m \times Cpaper$$

---

[1]Technically, this should have been drawn in the activity map as P → A, A → X. However, both the printer and copy machine are located in the assistant's office, and the time spent moving the computer printouts to the copy machine is small enough that we can assume the interaction is P → X without any damage to our model.

X → A Cost

Once the copies are done, the assistant gets ready to deliver them. Because the copy machine is in the assistant's office, this activity takes practically no time at all, and we can assume it is zero:

$$X \rightarrow A: 0$$

A → D, A → F, A → S Cost

Finally, the assistant delivers the survey results to the department Chair, faculty, and students' mailboxes. The cost is all distribution related and is a function of the assistant's wage rate (Wa) multiplied by the time it takes to distribute the survey results to the department Chair, faculty, and students' mailboxes (Tgivetochair, Tgivetofaculty, Tgivetostudents, respectively):

$$A \rightarrow D: Wa \times Tgivetochair$$

$$A \rightarrow F: Wa \times Tgivetofaculty$$

$$A \rightarrow S: Wa \times Tgivetostudents$$

To complete our interaction cost model, we need to assign initial values to the variables in the cost equations (see Figure 11-6). We then program the equations into our interaction matrix in Figure 11-7. We are now ready for diagnosis.

CONTROL PANEL:		units	comment
Wa	$ 15.00	per hour	Assistant's Wage Rate
Wg	$ -	per hour	Gopher's Wage Rate
Cfolder	$ 0.05		5 cents
Cpaper	$ 0.01		penny
Copportunity	$ -		Opportunity Cost
n	64	courses	each mini
m	45	students	in each course
avgReportSize	2	pages	per class
avgSummarySize	5	pages	overall
Tcopysurveys	1.00	hours	1 hour
Tpackagesurveys	0.50	hours	30 minutes
Tgetgophers	1.00	hours	1 hour
Tdistributesurveys	0.17	hours	10 minutes
Tcollectsurveys	0.17	hours	10 minutes
Treturnsurveys	0.08		5 minutes
Tentersurvey	0.25	hours	15 minutes per survey
Tgivetochair	0.08		5 minutes
Tgivetofaculty	0.08		5 miutes
Tgivetostudents	0.08		5 minutes

Figure 11-6. *Initial variable values*

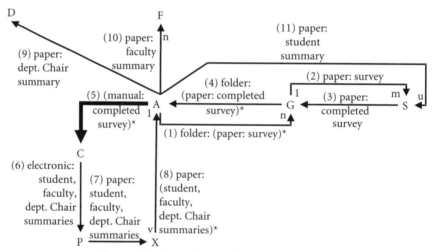

Figure 11-7. *Interaction matrix*

Step 3: Diagnose the Survey Activity

Over the course of a year, the course survey activity can cost over $60,000. By visual inspection, it is clear that the costs are localized around the A → C interaction, which contains 98% ($10,8000/$11,021.14) of the costs. This is clearly a time-intensive activity, and it can take the assistant up to a month to enter the data for the entire class. We want to design a treatment that eliminates the A → C interaction, and its associated costs (see Figure 11-8).

Figure 11-8. *The problematic interaction*

Step 4: Design Treatments

One possible treatment is to substitute the Web for the computer and all the agents that distribute and collect surveys (see Figure 11-9).

Note that this substitution eliminates the interactions A → G, G → S, S → G, G → A, and most importantly, A → C. A medium substitution is also needed; the students must enter their survey responses on the Web instead of on paper. What's nice about this solution is that the students can enter their information at their convenience; valuable class time no longer needs to be taken up with surveying activities.

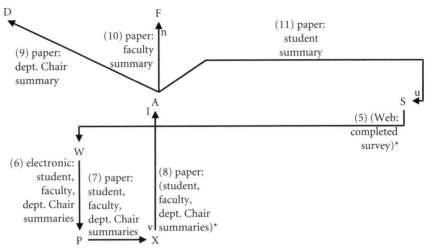

Figure 11-9. *Web-based course survey (actual implementation)*

Determining the value of this treatment is straightforward; we can reuse most of the original interaction matrix with the following changes (as seen in Figure 11-10). For each interaction eliminated, a zero is inserted into its cell in the interaction matrix, which has the effect of eliminating the costs of that interaction. Next, we replace the label for the computer (C) with the Web (W). The final step is to derive a cost equation for the students entering their survey information into the Web: S → W. However, because the students fill out the survey during their free time *and* DCE doesn't pay the students for this time, the cost of this interaction (to DCE) is zero.

In particular, by having students enter the information directly into the Web, the costs of the survey activity have been reduced an order of magnitude (from $66,126.84 down to $909.84 a year), for a savings of $65,217. We've accomplished our goal of an order of magnitude reduction without having to put the entire surveying activity online. What is the value of this treatment to DCE? First we need to figure out the treatment's costs.

Since the Department of Computational Ecology is at a major university, there are many computers around that can act as Web servers. Thus, the primary

INTERACTION MATRIX:

FROM/TO	A	G	S	W	P	X	D	F
A		0	$ 1.25		0		$ 1.25	$ 1.25
G	0			0				
S		0		0				
W					$ 1.33			
P						$ 148.56		
X	$ -							
D								
F								

SUMMARY:

	MINI	YEARLY
	$ 151.64	$ 909.84
ORIGINAL		$ 66,126.84
REDUCTION		98.62%
SAVINGS		$ 65,217.00

Figure 11-10. *The treatment's interaction matrix*

	YEAR 0	YEAR 1	YEAR 2	YEAR 3
BENEFITS	0	$ 65,217.00	$ 65,217.00	$ 65,217.00
COSTS	$ 10,000.00	$ -	$ -	$ -
PROFITS	$ (10,000.00)	$ 65,217.00	$ 65,217.00	$ 65,217.00
CASH FLOW	$ (10,000.00)	$ 56,710.43	$ 49,313.42	$ 42,881.24
NPV		$ 46,710.43	$ 96,023.86	$ 138,905.09
ROI		467%	960%	1389%

Figure 11-11.   *The value of our Web treatment over several years*

costs are your consultation and development fees. Let's assume this is $10,000. The value of the Web course survey treatment in terms of ROI can now be determined (see Figure 11-11).

Over three years, the Web course survey gives DCE an ROI of 1389% with a first year ROI of 467%[2]—all without putting the entire activity online. If the Chair, faculty, and students would accept online survey results (see Figure 11-12), then the cost of this activity could effectively be reduced to zero. This solution is left as an exercise for the reader.

What's important to note is that the partial Web-based solution still results in an order of magnitude improvement over the old activity. It isn't necessary to put the entire course survey online. To the uninitiated, handling a paper-based procedure on the Web means totally eliminating any paper used in the activity. And without applying a technique like Web Business Engineering, it's not clear what the benefits are of a partial Web solution; you have to adopt the fully paperless implementation just to be sure. However, with Web Business Engineering you can quantify the benefits of a partial Web solution, and if the benefits meet your metrics (in our case, an order of magnitude decrease in costs), then you don't have to waste time and money implementing the full solution.

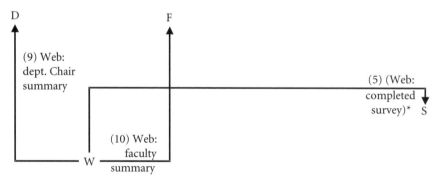

Figure 11-12.   *The fully Webbed course survey solution not implemented*

---

[2]Assumes a 15% discount rate; taxes and depreciation ignored.

CHAPTER TWELVE

WBE in Social/Cultural Situations: The Case of the Online Matchmaking Service

Executive Summary

Despite the name, Web Business Engineering is not just for businesses. One can use WBE to identify ways of using the Web to support social and, more generally, cultural activities, so long as information is a key part of those activities. Applying WBE in this manner is not too surprising considering that businesses are kinds of cultures in their own right. Thus, using WBE to analyze business activities is a kind of cultural activity analysis. One such cultural activity is date seeking, which is something in which virtually everyone participates at some point in their lives. As such, many offline social activities exist to help single people meet other singles. Not surprisingly, there are a growing number of Web sites as well. Unfortunately, most of these Web sites are based on the "Web as electronic paper" concept and therefore don't fully exploit the potential of online media to assist in dating. This chapter presents a detailed example of how one can use WBE to better use online media to support the dating activity.

Objectives

After reading this chapter you should be able to:

- *Apply Web Business Engineering to support cultural activities, which are information intensive*

- *Handle variables that are difficult to quantify in your value model such as opportunity and rejection costs*

- *Design advanced treatments that distribute content and proactively make that content explicit*

- *Design advanced treatments that use proactive reminders*

Introduction

Up to this point we've primarily looked at how Web Business Engineering could be used as a tool to support business activities. However, the popularity of chat rooms and message boards shows that the Web is a popular cultural tool as well. Can one apply Web Business Engineering to find good ways of using the Web to support cultural activities as well? The answer is a qualified "Yes!" So long as the activity studied is information intensive, you should have no problems applying Web Business Engineering to it. In this chapter we apply Web Business Engineering to a particular cultural activity: searching for a date.

There are two common ways people find dates "offline." They (1) go to a location where they have a high probability of meeting people, such as a party or club, or (2) use the personal ads in a local newspaper. We'll focus on the latter, but it's instructive to understand how a person finds dates in a club or other social gathering, since newspaper matchmaking emerged as an alternative to club dating.

The person looking for a date (hereafter, *date seeker,* or *seeker* for short) goes to some place where there is a high probability of finding a date, such as a party, club, or pub. Upon arrival, the seeker looks around for potential dates, people that he or she feels are attractive, approachable, unattached, and/or are somehow compatible. When a potential date is located, the seeker attempts to strike up a conversation with that person. During this initial conversation, different "pickup" lines may be used as a quick test for mutual interest, such as "I noticed you have the most beautiful eyes." Nonverbal techniques may also be used to check for inter-est—for example, the seeker may smile at the potential date and gauge interest by how he or she reacts. If the potential date does show an interest—usually by *not* telling the seeker to "get lost"—further conversation ensues, aimed at determining if there is good compatibility across one or more dimensions (physical, intellectual, political, or sexual). If so, the seeker asks for the potential date's phone number and promises to call at a later time. If and when the seeker does call, more compatibility discussion takes place, culminating in the couple agreeing on a time and place for a date. During the date, yet more compatibility-related discussions take place. If the couple decides they are indeed compatible, more dates follow. This entire activity continues over and over across different partners until the reason for seeking is met, such as marriage, sex, or friendship, to name a few.

Although some people find this activity enjoyable, for most finding a date in a club can be very expensive not only in terms of time, effort, and money but emotionally as well. For these reasons, newspaper personal ads emerged as an alternative to finding dates at clubs. In the following, we apply Web Business Engineering to discover ways of using the Web for finding a date. Consistent with Web Business Engineering's philosophy of using offline activities to drive online activities, we analyze how people use newspaper personal ads to find dates "offline." Based on this analysis, we derive several high value ways of finding dates that exploit the unique properties of the Web.

Case Study: Background

People use the following procedure to find dates via newspapers personal ads. The date seeker (X) places a personal ad in the local newspaper by either mailing or phoning in a rough description of who he or she is *(personal profile)*, followed by a rough description *(seeking profile)* of the person (Y) being sought. The ad may also include additional information about the qualities Y must have, such as a nonsmoker that likes classical music. The ads are usually brief because newspapers charge a lot for long personal ads. For example, newspapers commonly give date seekers the first 25 words for some nominal amount like $15; additional words are charged at a premium—$1 per additional word. Thus, most date seekers try to keep their ads to 25 words or less. Codes have even evolved so that common phrases take up less space. An example of such a code would be SWM, which is an abbreviation for "single white male" and counts as one word. A typical personal ad looks like the one in Figure 12-1.

> SWM seeks SWF for a long-term relationship.
>
> Must be a nonsmoker and like pets. 12345

Figure 12-1. *A typical newspaper personal ad*

For anonymity and safety reasons, X cannot contact Y directly. Instead the ad usually ends with a voice-mailbox number (in our example above, 12345) that X can call. Finally, all personal ads go in the "Personals" section of the newspaper, a section devoted exclusively to personal ads.

To search for a date, X reads the "Personal Ads" section of the newspaper and makes a list of potential matches (Ys) whose seeking profile matches X's own personal profile. X usually makes the list by circling the personal ads of potential Ys. X then calls the voice-mailbox numbers of each person on this list, leaving a voice-mail with additional information about himself or herself as well as a phone number. Y listens to the messages. If Y likes X's message, then Y phones X. Over the phone a lengthy discussion ensues aimed largely at discovering compatibility. If both parties are mutually interested, they agree on a time and place for a date. We now have enough information to map the newspaper matchmaking activity.

Step 1: Map Newspaper Matchmaking

Step 1 is for the potential date (Y) to place a personal ad in the newspaper either by phoning or mailing in his or her personal information (see Figure 12-2). To simplify the diagram, we just show Y placing a personal ad, but X usually places a personal ad as well.

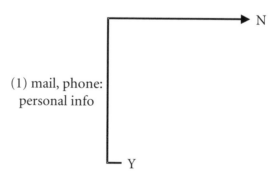

Figure 12-2.   *Placing personal information in the newspaper*

X reads the personal ads section (Step 2, Figure 12-3) of the paper and makes a list of potential dates by circling interesting personal ads in the newspaper.

For each person on the list, X calls their voice mailbox number (Step 3, Figure 12-4) and leaves a message. This message usually contains additional personal information about X as well as a phone number Y can call for further discussion. Y then listens to the messages (Step 4, Figure 12-4).

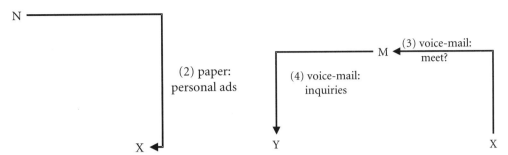

Figure 12-3. *Searching personal ads*   **Figure 12-4.** *Scheduling a potential date*

If Y likes X, then Y phones X (Step 5, Figure 12-5). The potential daters discuss compatibility issues and, if mutual interest results, where and when to go on a date.

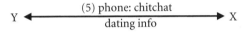

Figure 12-5. *Discussing dating details on the phone*

The final step (6) is to go out on a date (see Figure 12-6).

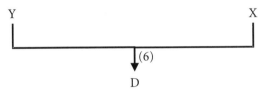

Figure 12-6. *Going out on a date*

The entire activity can be depicted as in Figure 12-7.

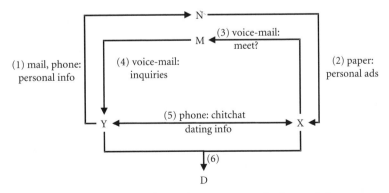

Figure 12-7. *The entire newspaper dating activity*

Step 2: Value Newspaper Matchmaking

As you probably have a good idea of the interactions in newspaper matchmaking, rather than explain each one in detail, a summary of the various cost equations appears in Figure 12-8.

	STEP 1	
X→N (depicted as Y→N in the above diagram)	\$paper+\$envelope+\$stamp+	Cost of the paper, envelope, and stamp for your personal ad
	$(T_{DevelopAd} + T_{PackageAd}) * \$O_x +$	Cost of developing and putting the personal ad in an envelope
	$T_{Mail} * \$O_x +\$fee$	Cost of going to the mailbox and mailing the personal ad
	STEP 2	
N→X	$T_{ReadAds} * \$O_x$	Cost of reading the paper looking for a match
	STEP 3	
X→M	$(T_{DevelopVoiceMail} + T_{SpeakVoiceMail}) * \$O_x$	Cost of developing what you want to say and the cost of speaking it on the phone
	STEP 4	
M→X	$T_{VoiceMailListen} * \$O_x$	Cost of listening to voice mail inquiries
	STEP 5	
X→Y Y←X	$T_{PhoneTalk} * \$O_x +$ $T_{PhoneListen} * \$O_x +$ \$R2x	Cost of talking on the phone Cost of listening on the phone Rejection cost

Figure 12-8. *Cost equations for newspaper matchmaking*

Now the problem with modeling these costs is that it is very difficult to quantify opportunity (\$Ox) and rejection costs (\$R2x), since they can vary tremendously among individuals. For example, a stock trader spending time looking for a date probably has a much higher opportunity cost than a teenager looking for a date. Similarly, due to lack of maturity, younger date seekers may have higher rejection costs than older ones. Thus, our model can never give us an absolute value for date seeking that applies to all people.

There are two ways around this problem, which is the more general problem of dealing with unquantifiable or *qualitative costs*. First, you ignore qualitative costs altogether; don't even include them in your model. But this isn't wise. Even though you can't quantify these costs, they are real and somehow need to be dealt with. Therefore, the second, and more preferable, approach is to keep them in your value model but minimize their effects by either setting them to zero, if they are added to an expression (such as $R2x), or to one, if they multiply some expression (such as $Ox). Then, in the diagnosis and treatment steps, try to design Web treatments that reduce or eliminate these factors. We'll do the latter, setting $R2x=0 and $Ox=1. In making these assumptions our interaction cost model essentially becomes a "best-case" model of the costs associated with newspaper matchmaking.

To complete our model, let's decide on some initial values for the variables in our cost equations. First, we'll set the time it takes to package (T_package_ad) and mail a personal ad (Tmail) to 1 and 10 minutes, respectively. This takes care of the times associated with placing a personal ad. Next, we'll set the time it takes a date seeker to read newspaper personal ads (TreadAds), develop a voice-mail message (TdevelopVoiceMail), send voice-mail messages (TspeakVoiceMail), and listen to voice-mail messages (TvoiceMailListen) to 30, 15, 5, and 10 minutes, respectively. Finally, we'll set the time it takes to chat on the phone with a potential date (TphoneTalk, TphoneListen) to 30 minutes, 15 minutes apiece for listening and talking. For monetary costs, we'll set paper, envelope, and stamp to 5 cents, 10 cents, and 33 cents, respectively (see Figure 12-9).

CONTROL PANEL:		units	comment
TdevelopAd	0.50	hours	30 minutes
T_package_ad	0.02	hours	1 minute
Tmail	0.17	hours	10 minutes
TreadAds	0.50	hours	30 minutes
TdevelopVoicemail	0.25	hours	15 minutes
TspeakVoicemail	0.08	hours	5 minutes
TvoicemailListen	0.17	hours	10 minutes
TphoneTalk	0.25	hours	15 minutes
TphoneListen	0.25	hours	15 minutes
$paper	$ 0.05		5 cents
$envelope	$ 0.10		10 cents
$stamp	$ 0.33		33 cents
$fee	$ 15.00		per week
$Ox	$ 1.00		
$R2x	$ -		

Figure 12-9. *Initial variable values*

INTERACTION MATRIX:						SUMMARY:		
FROM/TO	X	Y	M	N		1-Week		1-Year
X		$ 0.50	$ 0.33	$ 16.16		$ 17.66		$ 918.49
Y								
M	$ 0.17							
N	$ 0.50							

Figure 12-10. *Interaction matrix for newspaper date seeking*

With our initial values set, we can program our cost equations (see Figure 12-8) into an interaction matrix (see Figure 12-10). Our interaction-cost model shows that at minimum, the cost of newspaper matchmaking is $918.49 a year. Next we try to determine what drives this cost.

Step 3: Diagnose Newspaper Matchmaking

Using the one-half value heuristic on the time variables shows that none of them have a big effect on costs (see Figure 12-11). As one would expect, you get the biggest savings (1.42%) from reducing the most time-intensive activities such as time spent developing the personal ad and the time spent reading personal ads. All other time variables result in less than a 1% savings when applying the one-half value heuristic. The biggest cost driver is the fee to place a personal ad. Cutting that value in half results in a 42% savings. As a final note, cutting opportunity cost (Ox) in half results in only a 6% cost savings.

So, unlike the course survey case from the last chapter, there are no cost drivers that can be eliminated to result in order of magnitude improvements. In these situations, handling a single portion of the activity online is probably not as good as placing the entire activity online. Therefore, our goal in designing a treatment is to use the Web to support the entire activity, minimizing the cost of each interaction.

CONTROL PANEL:		units	comment	1/2-savings
TdevelopAd	0.50	hours	30 minutes	1.42%
T_package_ad	0.02	hours	1 minute	0.05%
Tmail	0.17	hours	10 minutes	0.47%
TreadAds	0.50	hours	30 minutes	1.42%
TdevelopVoicemail	0.25	hours	15 minutes	0.71%
TspeakVoicemail	0.08	hours	5 minutes	0.24%
TvoicemailListen	0.17	hours	10 minutes	0.47%
TphoneTalk	0.25	hours	15 minutes	0.71%
TphoneListen	0.25	hours	15 minutes	0.71%
$paper	$ 0.05		5 cents	0.14%
$envelope	$ 0.10		10 cents	0.28%
$stamp	$ 0.33		33 cents	0.93%
$fee	$ 15.00		per week	42.00%
$Ox	$ 1.00			6.18%
$R2x	$ -			

Figure 12-11. *Savings from applying the one-half heuristic*

Furthermore, our treatment should concentrate on eliminating or minimizing the effects of the qualitative variables such as opportunity and rejection cost.

Step 4: Design Treatments for Newspaper Matchmaking

Up to this point, we've discussed two kinds of treatments: agent substitutions and media substitutions. The Web solutions you design using such treatments are still very similar to the offline activities on which they're based. However, there are two other treatments you can perform that take advantage of the unique properties of online media and that result in Web solutions that are very different from their offline counterparts. The treatments are *add pro-activity* and *distribute content*. We apply all these substitutions to our activity map. To illustrate an actual implementation of these substitutions, screen dumps from the Web site *http://www.datingexpert.com* are used. In fact, the Dating Expert Web site was created using all these substitutions. We start with the original map in Figure 12-12 and then apply the five treatments below.

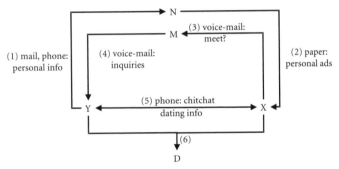

Figure 12-12.   *The original activity map for newspaper matchmaking*

Treatment 1: Substitute Agents

The first treatment is to replace all intermediate agents with the Web (see underlined agents in Figure 12-13). We do this by taking the newspaper (N) and voicemail (M) and replacing them with one agent: the Web (W). The information that used to go to these agents is then routed to the Web (see Figure 12-14).

However, the media requirements for the Web are different from those of the original agents—in particular, the Web cannot take down personal information over the phone (Step 1). We need to apply several media substitutions in order for this agent substitution to work.

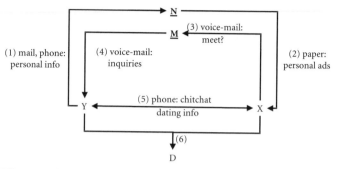

Figure 12-13.   *Before Treatment 1. The Web will replace the underlined agents*

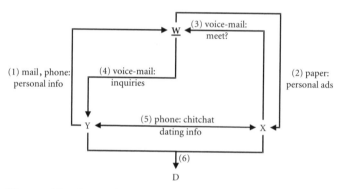

Figure 12-14.   *After Treatment 1. Newspaper and voice-mail replaced by the Web*

Treatment 2: Substituting Media

In our activity map, some form of Web media must replace the media in Step 1 through Step 4 (see Figure 12-15). Additionally, although not necessary, you should also examine ways of substituting Web media for the remaining media in the map. For example, Step 5 was unaffected by the Web substitution. However, you should still examine the interaction and determine if you can substitute Web media for the phone. Remember, our goal throughout this treatment is to keep the same content but deliver it over different, *Web,* media.

Rather than just talk about the substitutions we are going to make, let's look at actual examples of media substitutions to highlight the tremendous flexibility and power of Web media. We'll look at substitutions for each interaction (step) in our activity map.

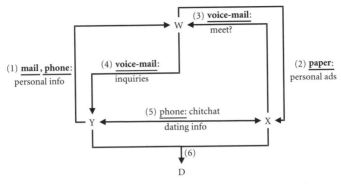

Figure 12-15. *Before Treatment 2. Media that must be substituted with Web media are boldfaced*

Web Media Substitutions for Step 1: Form-Based Personal Ads and Online Payment Forms

Instead of mailing information into the newspaper, both the personal profile (see Figure 12-16) and seeking profile (see Figure 12-17) can be entered into a Web-based (online) form. By putting personal and seeking profiles online, mailing costs are eliminated. Furthermore, the use of drop-down boxes for the various categories in the personal and seeking profiles reduces the time it takes to place a personal ad. Payment can be sent via an online form as well (see Figure 12-18).

Figure 12-16. *Web-based personal profile*

Figure 12-17. *Personal ad: seeking profile*

Figure 12-18. *Online payment*

Web Media Substitutions for Step 2: Smart Search Forms and Filtered Listings

Just as with a newspaper, date seekers can search through a Web page of personal ads. However, the Web allows more efficient searches than a newspaper. For example, instead of the date seeker scrolling through a large number of listings, he or she can enter a seeking profile into a form (see Figure 12-19). When the date seeker hits the "Find Matches" button, the site only returns the names of those users that fit the date seeker's criteria (see Figure 12-20). Thus, the seeker does not waste time looking through inappropriate listings; each name returned is a good match.

Figure 12-19. *Smart search through personal ads*

Because each name is a good match, the potential date's information does not have to be shown. If the date seeker wants to see more information about a potential date, they can click on the potential date's name (see Figure 12-21).

Figure 12-20. *Smart listing of potential dates*

Figure 12-21. *Detailed personal ad for a potential date*

Web Media for Step 3: Private Mailboxes

In newspaper matchmaking, if the date seeker finds a potential date, he or she sends a message to the person's voice-mailbox either requesting further information or to set a date and time for a future phone conversation. We can replace the voice-mailbox with a private mailbox on the dating Web site. If the date seeker is still interested at this point, he or she can send an e-mail requesting further information or a meeting (Figure 12-22).

Figure 12-22. *Sending mail to a private mailbox*

Web Media for Step 4: Mailbox Listings

Besides serving as a communication tool, the voice-mailbox in newspaper matchmaking hides the identity of the date seekers (for obvious security reasons). To maintain anonymity, each user on the Dating Expert Web site is given a secret name and a private mailbox. Any communication between potential dates is sent to this private mailbox on the Dating Expert Web site (see Figure 12-23). However, instead of having to listen to a bunch of phone messages, the date seeker can quickly see how many messages he or she has and read them.

Figure 12-23.   *Private mailbox*

Web Media for Step 5: Chat, Instant Messaging

In newspaper matchmaking, if two people decide there is enough common interest, they agree to talk on the phone. There is no reason for Web date seekers to limit themselves to just this medium. There are other Web media they can use such as chat or instant messaging (screen dump not shown). These Web communications media eliminate a lot of the awkwardness associated with communicating with a relative stranger over the phone. Finally, it is important to note that when you substitute Web media, if it's possible to keep the old medium, do so. There is no reason, for example, to eliminate the phone. If the date seekers want to talk over the phone, that should still be an option. Thus, the entire activity has been changed as shown in Figure 12-24.

Timewise, this new Web-based activity is better because date seekers can more quickly compose personal ads (Step 1), search through personal ads (Step 2), and view potential dates (Step 4).

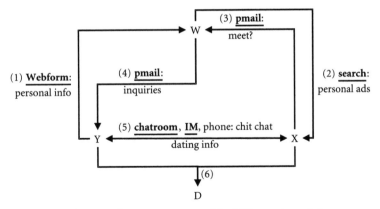

Figure 12-24. *After Treatment 2. The Web version of the newspaper matchmaking*

Treatment 3: Distribute and Proactively Make Content Explicit

We have used the Web to make two of the three "time sinks" more efficient, namely filling out the personal ad and searching the personal ad listings. However, another big time sink occurred in Step 5, the lengthy phone discussion between the date seeker and potential date (see Figure 12-25). Recall that for the date seekers, one of the primary goals of this discussion is to determine compatibility, as personal ads provide only a superficial glimpse of a person (marital status, race, gender, age) and only after compatibility is established do the date seekers spend time planning the date.

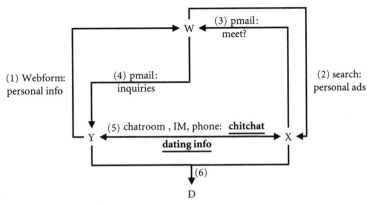

Figure 12-25. *Before Treatment 3. Implicit information that needs to be distributed is boldfaced*

The Web should have a way of making such compatibility information explicit. The general idea is to *identify areas on the map where implicit information is transformed into explicit information, then use the Web to make that information explicit earlier in the activity.* For example, take the compatibility discussion. Compatibility discussions could be shorter if the date seekers knew more about each other ahead of time. But this statement seems to present a paradox: How can you know more about a person without speaking to him or her first? The answer is to properly exploit the interactive and *proactive* capabilities of the Web. The latter is the ability of the Web to provide information automatically, without the user directly asking for it. First let's examine how to use the Web's interactive capabilities to make compatibility information more explicit.

One way an online matchmaking service can exploit the interactive capabilities of the Web is by having compatibility tests that the date seeker can optionally fill out when he or she places a personal ad (see Figure 12-26). One problem with these tests is that they can be fairly long and they delay the user from doing his or her primary task: finding a date.

Figure 12-26. *An example of a scientific compatibility test*

Besides forcing the user to fill out compatibility tests, a Web matchmaking service can use less intrusive compatibility mechanisms, which exploit the proactive capabilities of the Web. For example, many date seekers use techniques like astrology and numerology to determine compatibility (the latter uses a person's name or birth date to derive a "magic number" that supposedly says something about that person's personality). The Web can automatically calculate this information based on the information the user enters when he or she initially fills out a personal ad.[1]

In the Dating Expert Web site, for example, when reading a potential date's personal profile, the astrological sign of that person appears as well as an interpretation of that sign's compatibility with the date seeker's sign (see Figure 12-27). The potential date's magic number is also given along with the personality interpretation associated with that number. Finally, if both date seeker and potential date have filled out the optional scientific personality test, then the results of their personality compatibility are also displayed.

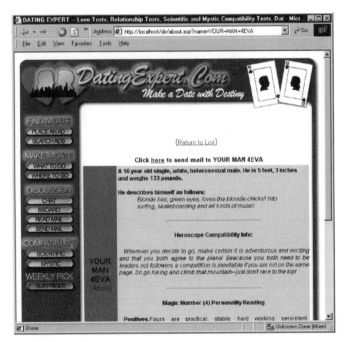

Figure 12-27.   *Compatibility test results automatically incorporated in the personal ads*

---

[1]Whether these tests are valid is not the point. The point is that many date seekers rely on them.

What the Web has essentially done is taken information that used to be discussed in Step 5—chitchat—and distributed this information earlier in the activity, Steps 1 and 2. You can imagine taking the dating information and distributing that earlier as well. For example, when sending personal mail to a potential date (Step 3), a date seeker can mark a set of dates and times he or she is available onto a Web calendar. That calendar gets attached to the recipient's mail message (Step 4).

By having the Web play a proactive role in automatically running these tests and displaying their results early in the activity, this information is made more explicit to date seekers, and they don't have to spend as much time discussing them (Figure 12-28).

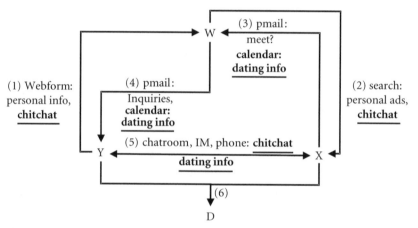

Figure 12-28.   *After Treatment 3. Chitchat and dating information are distributed earlier in the process and made more explicit*

Treatment 4: Use Proactive Reminders

Much attention is given to the Web's interactive, multimedia capabilities. However, just as important and often overlooked are the Web's proactive capabilities. We've already seen one demonstration of the Web's proactive capabilities in treatment 3, where the Web automatically computed compatibility information and made this information available earlier in the activity. Another powerful, proactive capability is the Web's ability to automatically send reminders to users.

Specifically, note that users don't have to interact with the Web in order to get information back. For example, date seekers don't have to remember to periodically check their private mailboxes for messages. Instead, the Web can remind users to check their mailboxes only when new messages arrive. Indeed, in Dating

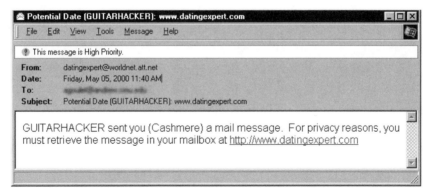

Figure 12-29. *Users receive reminders to check their private mailboxes on Dating Expert via their actual e-mail*

Expert, we have implemented a mechanism whereby date seekers are notified via their actual e-mail about new messages in their private mailbox (Figure 12-29).

The general rule is *use the Web's proactive capabilities to support those information activities that require the user to remember something.* By exploiting the Web's proactive capabilities, the timing of activities becomes more efficient, as in our example of the Dating Expert mailbox reminder (see Figure 12-30).

We now have an online matchmaking service based on newspaper personal ads that clearly reduces many of the latter's time-consuming activities. Furthermore, the timing of activities is more efficient because the Web proactively

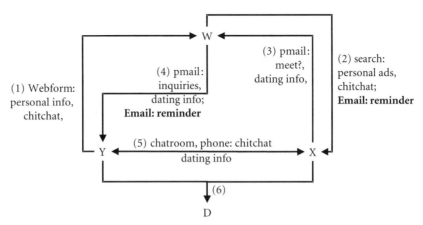

Figure 12-30. *After Treatment 3. Proactively reminding users to check their private mailboxes only when necessary*

reminds users to visit the site only when necessary. By reducing the time spent in date-seeking activities as well as improving the timing of these activities, the effects of opportunity cost are reduced. Finally, precomputing compatibility information and automatically displaying these results early in the activity minimizes the likelihood of being rejected, so rejection costs are minimized. Thus, although we cannot quantify opportunity and rejection, through various treatments we can minimize the factors they most strongly affect—such as time—which in turn minimizes their overall effect on the activity.

In closing, remember that you are not haphazardly developing a business Web site or application. We use Web Business Engineering to systematically design online treatments based on a value model of some offline activity, even when we cannot quantify all the factors in this model. Now, although Web Business Engineering uses offline activities as the basis for online ones, you shouldn't be afraid to add information and other mechanisms that don't appear offline. However, this kind of content should only be added after you've properly supported the offline activity online (see Figure 12-31).

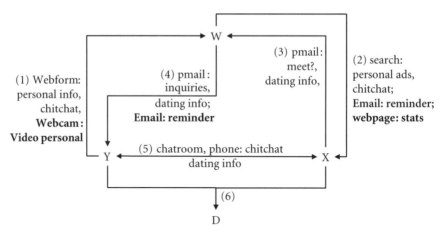

Figure 12-31.   *An example of novel content (**bold type**) added only after properly supporting the offline activity*

Up to this point, we've applied Web Business Engineering to analyze and support offline activities online. However, you can use Web Business Engineering to analyze and improve online activities as well. We explore this use in the final section.

Case Studies: Applying Web Business Engineering to Online Activities

We have discussed Web Business Engineering (WBE) as a means of discovering high-value ways of handling offline activities online. Most of this material was targeted at Web consultants, although Web entrepreneurs could use the concepts to develop their business Web sites. In this section, we examine ways of using Web Business Engineering to analyze and improve online activities. Our goal is mainly to discover innovations, so we focus primarily on mapping (Step 1) and treating (Step 4) of online activities. In Chapter 13, we use Web Business Engineering to analyze ten existing online mechanisms for driving traffic to Web sites and use the results to design a new mechanism for inexpensively driving traffic to a Web site. Chapter 14 uses Web Business Engineering to derive a theory of Memetic Marketing. In this theory, your Web site is viewed as a collection of memes—the information equivalent of a gene—and if you want to drive large volumes of traffic to your site with little effort and expense, you must design an effective replicator. Finally, Chapter 15 applies Web Business Engineering to the problem of maximizing the money your site makes. It introduces the concept of information-currency and explains that to maximize your site's revenues, you must demand different kinds of payment depending on how the user perceives the risk and value of your Web site's content. The discussion is based on the case in Chapter 12, so if you haven't read it, you should do so before reading Chapter 15. Web entrepreneurs will find the material in this section especially valuable, but Web consultants should be able to apply the concepts to their client's Web sites as well.

CHAPTER THIRTEEN

Marketing Your Web Site

Executive Summary

One can use Web Business Engineering (WBE) to develop a high-value-added online business, but a great Web business alone does not guarantee success. Ultimately, a Web business needs traffic. Fortunately, one can also use WBE to discover ways to drive traffic to a Web business. In this chapter, we use WBE to map out existing ways of driving traffic to Web sites, with an emphasis on *low-cost* ways of generating traffic. From these maps we generalize the key requirements for driving traffic to a Web site. We then use WBE to invent a new way of *inexpensively* marketing one's Web business.

Objectives

After reading this chapter you should be able to

- *Apply Web Business Engineering to map online activities*

- *Employ Web Business Engineering for marketing purposes*

Introduction

Imagine you have a great idea for a Web business (P). You apply Web Business Engineering and develop a Web site (W) with great content and several revenue-generating mechanisms. Next, you register a domain name and buy space with an Internet service provider. Finally, you upload your site's content and wait for the customers (C) to visit and the money to roll in. Unfortunately, what typically happens is your Web site sits there, generating hardly any money at all (see Figure 13-1). The problem is that it's simply not enough to implement a great Web site; you have to make people aware of your Web site. This is where marketing comes in. Marketing is the activity that brings consumers to your Web site and makes them want to purchase your content. If you want a successful Web site, you must engage in marketing.

There are many different ways to market your Web site. Let's first look at conventional (offline) ways to do it. Using WBE mapping, we can depict conventional marketing as shown in Figure 13-2. Conventional marketing uses radio, television, magazines, and other printed media to make people aware of your Web site's address and content. The key to successfully marketing your Web site through conventional means is to pick a medium (radio, television, print) and possibly a timeslot that reaches the maximum number of your target users. You then design a catchy advertisement and broadcast it in this medium. Although conceptually simple, a lot of skill is required to design a concise ad that gets people to remember both what services your Web site provides and its address. However, assuming you are successful, you can rely on traditional advertising statistics for support. For example, newspapers will boast a 2.5 percent response rate to advertisements, which means if the newspaper's readership is 1 million, you can expect 25,000 people to visit your Web site. Unfortunately, advertising in conventional media can be very expensive—typically costing thousands of dollars for a newspaper, radio, or magazine ad that runs for a week. What are the inexpensive alternatives?

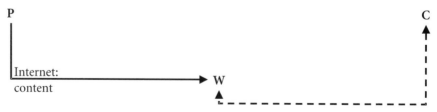

Figure 13-1.   *A Web site* without *marketing*

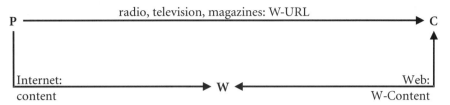

Figure 13-2. *Activity map for conventional marketing*

The Web, being a complex multimedia environment, should provide a number of different media that you can use to market your Web site. We'll use WBE to map out the information activity surrounding existing Web media (like search engines) that have emerged to support the marketing of Web businesses. We'll then combine these online maps with offline maps to come up with new ways of marketing Web businesses. First, however, let's see what the basic marketing problem looks like in terms of a WBE map (see Figure 13-3).

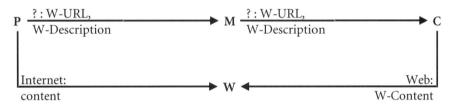

Figure 13-3. *The basic marketing problem*

The basic problem is coming up with a medium (M) that can convey both your Web site's address (URL) and a description of your Web site's services (W-Description). This medium should also make your Web site's information available when the user needs your services and starts looking for them.

Ten Free Ways of Generating Traffic

There are at least ten different ways that content providers drive traffic to their Web sites. We'll map each of these activities and list the benefits and drawbacks of each approach.

Search Engines

The most common way content providers (P) try to generate traffic is through search engines (S) (see Figure 13-4), such as *www.lycos.com, www.altavista.com,* and *www.hotbot.com.* First, P sends his or her Web site's address (W-URL) to S via

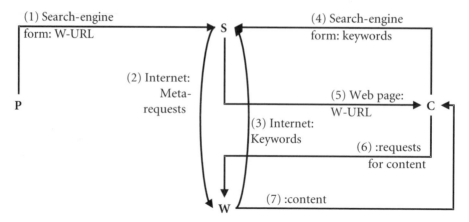

Figure 13-4. *Generating traffic via search engines*

a Web form (Step 1). S sends a "spider"—an automatic program that analyzes a Web site's content—to visit P's Web site (W) and categorizes its content (Steps 2 and 3). When a customer (C) visits S and submits keywords that are related to W's content (Step 4), S returns W's URL (W-URL) along with the URLs of other Web sites with content related to C's keywords. If C clicks on W-URL, he or she is directed to W (Steps 6 and 7).

The benefits of using a search engine to generate traffic are twofold. First, search engines are the first things users try when they're looking for Web content. Second, the traffic that search engines drive to your site are usually your target customers. If C visits your Web site via a search engine, it is highly likely that he or she is looking for content that you provide and thus will engage in a transaction.

There are several drawbacks with search engines. One is that the time to categorize W can be very long (Steps 2 and 3)—several weeks for some search engines. Second, the chance of C visiting W (Steps 6 and 7) can be very low. This is especially true if there are many Web sites related to C's keywords (Step 4), in which case the list of URLs returned (Step 5) will be very long, and W-URL may be at the bottom. It takes a lot of work to structure the content of your page—which includes the <META> tags—so that W-URL appears high up in the search listing pages.

Search Directories

A variation on search engines is the search directory (see Figure 13-5). Search engines and search directories are the most common search instruments Web users employ when trying to find content. Examples of search directories are *www.yahoo.com, www.dmoz.org,* and *www.about.com.* Similar to a search engine, the content provider (P) submits a URL (W-URL) to the search directory (D). Additionally, P provides a brief description (W-Description) about his or her Web site (W) (Step 1). Step 2 is where search directories differ from search engines. Instead of sending a spider to automatically categorize the Web site, a number of human editors (H) go through the list of submitted URLs (Step 2). H manually examine W's content and assign W to the appropriate section of the directory (Step 5). When a consumer (C) visits D, he or she can either type in keywords and get a list of relevant URLs or search through the directory—which is arranged as a hierarchy of topics and subtopics—until he or she finds a relevant URL (Steps 6 and 7). If C clicks on W-URL, then he or she is directed to W (Steps 8 and 9).

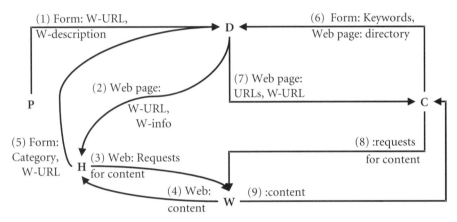

Figure 13-5. *Generating traffic through search directories*

One benefit of being in a search directory as opposed to a search engine is that the human editors screen out bad Web sites and only include those that they feel provide high value. So if you get in, your site usually appears high on the search results page. Another benefit is that the most popular search instrument on the Web is a search directory, namely, *www.yahoo.com.* Getting in this directory increases your chances of getting traffic. A final benefit is that more search instruments are starting to combine search directories and search engines, with the directory results appearing *before* the search engine results. So it pays to get listed in a search directory.

Unfortunately, a big drawback of using search directories to drive traffic to your Web site is that inclusion in the directory is a judgment call on the part of the human editor and the criteria for getting listed is typically not specified in detail. Furthermore, it can take several months before the editors review your Web site.

Banner Programs

Search engines and search directories are customer-initiated traffic-generating mechanisms. You only get traffic if the customer takes an active role in looking for your product and services. A more proactive mechanism is the banner program (see Figure 13-6). In the banner program the content provider (P) first submits a bitmap advertisement—analogous to a billboard—along with his or her Web site's (W) address (W-URL) and a brief description of the Web site's content (content-info). In exchange for showing P's banner, P agrees to show banners for other Web sites (Step 2, banner: V-URL). Each time W shows someone else's banner (Step 3), he or she gets a fraction of a credit, typically one-half credit (Step 4). If one of P's members (C) clicks on the banner, then P gets one full credit. When P gets one full credit, P's banner is shown on someone else's (V) Web site (Steps 5 to 7). Hopefully, C_W visits W (Step 8).

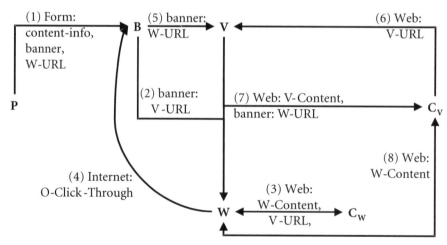

Figure 13-6. *Generating traffic through banner programs*

The benefit of banner advertising is that P is taking a more proactive role in getting customers instead of waiting for customers to come. Unfortunately, the drawbacks far outweigh the benefits of banner advertising. First, banners take up space on the user's screen that could be better served with W's content. Second, banners drive traffic away from P's Web site. Third, P has very little control over which Web sites P's banner is shown. Conversely, P has very little control over which banners are shown on W. The typical banner program only allows restrictions for adult material. As such, P's banner may be shown to users that are not part of his or her target demographics, and W may show banners that are inappropriate for P's target demographics.

Reality  Banner advertising accounts for only 0.63 percent of the traffic to my Web sites. On average, my students and I experience less than a 0.4 percent clickthrough rate when our banners are shown on other Web sites.

E-mail

A more proactive, direct way of advertising one's Web business is via e-mail (see Figure 13-7). To do this free of charge, content providers (P) must first go to a Web-based USENET newsgroup service (D) such as Deja News *(www.deja.com)*. USENET newsgroups can be thought of as online bulletin boards organized around various topics such as hobbies and sports. Users that post information to USENET include their e-mail addresses so that other users can follow up with them in private.

P can go to D and read postings from various topic groups related to the content of P's Web site (Step 1). From these postings, P can extract *leads* in the form of e-mail addresses (posting: eMail-C_i) and store them in the Web site's (W's) database (Step 2). P can then run a script on W to send the leads (C) e-mail with the Web site's URL (W-URL) and description (W-Description, Step 3). Hopefully the users will visit the Web site (Steps 4 and 5).

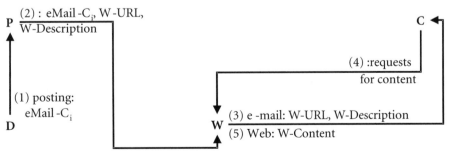

Figure 13-7. *E-mail direct marketing as a traffic-generating mechanism*

The drawbacks to this approach are that it can be tedious to manually create a big e-mail list. Furthermore, many customers view e-mail advertisements as spam, which can have negative consequences for W's image. Nevertheless, the benefits of being able to target a large number of relevant consumers cannot be overlooked.

Reality

My Web sites experience a 13 percent response rate for e-mail advertisements, which is about 10 times greater than direct-mail advertisements (1 to 2 percent response rate) and about 20 times better than printed ads (0.5 to 0.75 percent response rate).

Newsgroups

Besides advertising by creating e-mailing lists from newsgroups, the content provider can also advertise *within* newsgroups (see Figure 13-8). The content provider (P) simply posts a message containing his or her Web site's URL (W-URL) to a relevant USENET (U) newsgroup (Step 1). Usenet participants (C) read the message (Steps 2 and 3) and hopefully visit W (Steps 4 and 5).

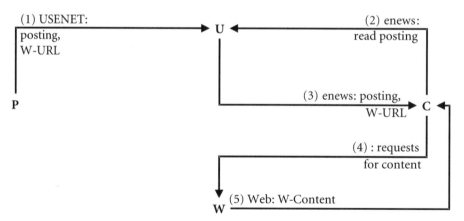

Figure 13-8. *Advertising in newsgroups*

Unlike banner advertising, newsgroup advertising allows P to target relevant consumers (C). Posting in a newsgroup has the added benefit that your advertisement will be around for a long time, as many services store several years worth of newsgroup postings that can be retrieved by keywords. However, the size of the newsgroup's community may be small, and there is no guarantee that all members of the community will read your message. Furthermore, it's against USENET etiquette to post advertisements, and even a single posting that looks like a pure advertisement may result in a nasty e-mail to P's Internet service provider (ISP), asking for the removal of P's account. As many ISPs have no-spam policies, this is not a threat to be taken lightly. The trick is for P to disguise the posting so that it does not seem like an advertisement—in other words, putting newsgroup-related information in the body of the posting and having the Web site's address as part of the poster's signature. P should also structure the wording of a posting so that it shows up high on the list when users do searches on past articles.

Reality  In my experience, expect a 1:4 response rate for newsgroup advertisements—that is, one posted newsgroup ad generates four responses.

Chats

One of the growing methods of advertising a Web site is through chat rooms (see Figure 13-9). The procedure is very similar to that of newsgroups except that the advertisements happens in real time. The content provider (P) simply goes to relevant rooms (R) in the various Internet chat sites and posts an advertisement in the form of a message along with the URL (W-URL) to P's Web site (Step 1). Users in the chat room who are engaged in conversation see the advertisement (Steps 2 and 3) and hopefully visit W (Steps 4 and 5).

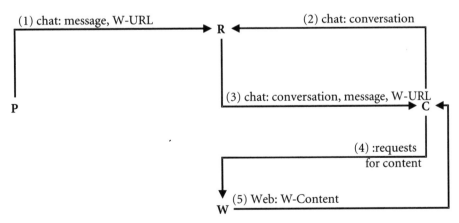

Figure 13-9.   *Chat room advertising*

Like newsgroups, chat rooms are organized according to topics. This allows P to enter specific rooms to target relevant consumers. However, unlike newsgroups the advertisement can quickly scroll off the screen, particularly if the room has a lot of conversation. Moreover, chat administrators can kick P out of rooms or even ban P from the chat site entirely. There are even automatic programs (chatbot administrators) that can kick users out of rooms if they post URLs. The final drawback is that the response rate from chat room advertisements is very low. However, the number of users in the most popular chat sites is in the tens of thousands, which makes chat advertising an attractive mechanism for generating traffic. There are two basic tricks to launching a successful chat advertising campaign. The first is to design a brief yet catchy message that makes users want to visit your Web site. The second, and most important, is to write a chatbot, a program that automatically visits the rooms you target and advertises your message.

Reality  In my experience, the response rate for chat rooms is 0.2 percent, which is pretty low. Paradoxically, chat room advertising brings in 38 percent of the traffic to my Web sites.

I have no experience with the next two ways of generating traffic, but they still deserve mention, as they are popular ones.

Web Rings

A Web ring is a collection of Web sites with related content (see Figure 13-10). The content provider (P) first locates a relevant Web ring (not shown, but Ps typically find Web rings via search engines). P then gets the Web ring code from the Web ring administrator (W_A) and places this code on his or her Web site's (W_p) front page (Steps 1 to 3). The code allows users visiting P's Web site to visit other Web sites by clicking on forward and backward buttons (there are also buttons for randomly visiting a Web site in the ring or for jumping forward or backward by several Web sites). This linear search mechanism is quite different from the random-access, keyword-based system employed by search engines. A user (C) visits one of the sites in the Web ring (W_i), not necessarily P's Web site (Step 4), and only by traversing the ring backward and forward (Step 5) does C eventually arrive at P's site.

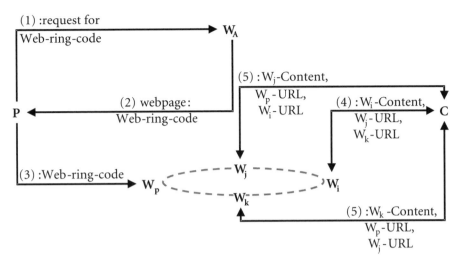

Figure 13-10. *Getting traffic from Web rings*

The primary benefit of using a Web ring is that the traffic visiting P's Web site is targeted. However, there are more drawbacks than benefits. By adding the Web ring code, P not only provides a mechanism for driving traffic out of his or her Web site, but, more devastating, it's a mechanism that drives traffic to a *competitor's* Web site. Also if C first visits a site that provides the content he or she is looking for, then C will probably not continue on to P's site. Web rings seem more appropriate for hobby sites, such as celebrity picture Web sites, rather than for serious Web businesses.

Top-N Web Sites

Top-N Web sites (W_N) provide consumers (C) a list of URLs with related content, not unlike the list of URLs returned by search engines (see Figure 13-11). However, W_N provides value by sorting the URLs according to popularity. A consumer (C) visits W_N and examines the list of URLs returned (Steps 2 and 3). When C clicks on one of the URLs on the list, a signal is sent to W_N to update the number of times that particular URL was visited, while C is simultaneously sent to W (Steps 4 and 5).

To use W_N for advertising, the content provider (P) first submits his or her URL (W-URL) to W_N (Step 1). P's Web site (W) is initially placed at the bottom of the list. If enough Cs click on W, then W rises in popularity, which is reflected by a higher listing on the results page.

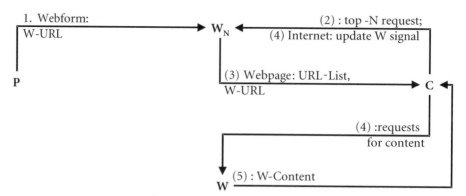

Figure 13-11. *Using Top-N Web sites to generate traffic*

The benefit of using a Top-N site to generate traffic is similar to that of a Web ring: P's site gets targeted traffic. However, Ps have no control over users clicking on their URLs beyond the brief description submitted. Another drawback is that all P's competitors are listed on the page as well. Like Web rings, Top-N advertising seems more appropriate for hobbyist sites rather than for Web businesses. Finally, let's look at non-online ways of generating traffic.

Picking a Good Web Site Name

A relatively simple and easy way to ensure some traffic to your Web site is to pick a good domain name (see Figure 13-12). Many users will opt to guess a company's URL before looking it up in a search engine (Steps 1 and 2). For example, if a user wants to find the Toys 'R' Us Web site, he or she will probably first try typing *www.toysrus.com* into his or her browser instead of going to a search engine and entering "Toys 'R' Us" as a keyword. In general, if you've either developed a brand, a well-known trademark, or a very focused product or service, your Web site's name should definitely reflect this information.

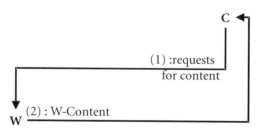

Figure 13-12. *Picking a good Web site name*

The benefit of picking a good Web site name is that users can quickly find you and do so in a "natural" manner. Furthermore, C is actually looking for W, so the traffic driven to W is targeted. The obvious drawback to anyone who has tried this approach is that all the good domain names are taken. For example, if you have a company that manufactures widgets, it is highly unlikely that you can register *www.widgets.com* as your domain name, unless you happened to register the name during the Web's infancy. Alarmingly, even trademarked names are taken by users that don't own them—cybersquatters—for the purposes of selling them back to their owners.

Reality  Only 1.3 percent of my Web sites' traffic is due to users guessing the site's address.

Word of Mouth

The final way of driving traffic is to have other people refer traffic to your Web site (see Figure 13-13). Suppose two friends (C, C_F) are talking, and during the conversation something triggers C_F's memory of your Web site (W) (Steps 1 and 2). C_F mentions this to C (Step 2), and at some later time C visits W (Steps 3 and 4).

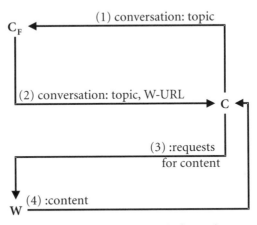

Figure 13-13. *Word of mouth*

This is the ultimate goal of any Web site: to have an existing customer bring in more customers. In this manner, the Web site can grow without any mediation by the content provider. The clear drawback to this approach is that if you haven't established a "presence," no one will refer you.

Reality ✔ Word of mouth referrals generate 3.8 percent of my Web site's traffic. This is better than individual search engines.

The Product

The product of these activities is obvious: customers. However, the product goes deeper than that. Ideally, you want each customer to know what product or service your Web business provides, as well as the location (URL/Web address) of your Web business, so that when they need your products or services, they automatically go to your Web site. If content providers could somehow "beam" this knowledge directly into the heads of all relevant consumers (Step 1), this is precisely the content they would relay (see Figure 13-14). So for the content provider (P), the problem boils down to finding who the relevant customers are and placing P's location and description of products/services into their heads.

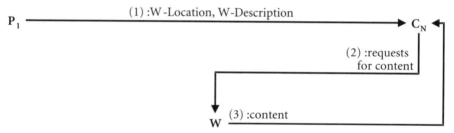

Figure 13-14.   *The ideal—albeit impractical—approach*

Unfortunately, until we have mass-thought-transfer technology, these ten mechanisms will have to go along with whatever other mechanisms we can come up with using WBE. To apply WBE to this problem, let's first map out a prototype activity.

Step 1: Map (Prototype) Activity

Based on the sequence and type of content exchanged, three distinct kinds of activities can be generalized from the preceding maps. The first is a brokered passive activity whereby the consumers (C) find the content provider (P) via a broker (B). Many different agents play the role of broker, which includes search engines, search directories, Top-10, Web rings, and other consumers. We can generalize the activity maps as follows (see Figure 13-15).

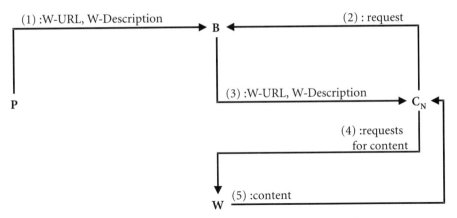

Figure 13-15. *The brokered, passive approach*

The second activity is where P takes a proactive role and uses a broker like a newsgroup, chat site, or banner program to advertise directly to consumers (see Figure 13-16). The main difference between this map and the brokered-passive map (see Figure 13-15) is that the user may not be specifically looking for W.

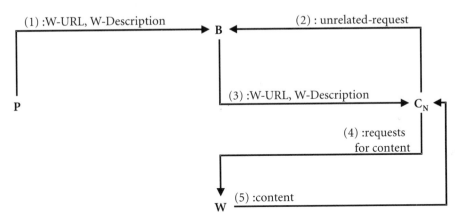

Figure 13-16. *The brokered, proactive approach*

The third activity is where P takes a proactive role and uses a broker (L) to get C's contact information, which P then uses to advertise directly to C via W (see Figure 13-17). The example given was e-mail direct marketing.

With our prototype activities mapped, let's try to find new ways of driving traffic to our Web site. Because our primary interest is innovation and not improvement, we skip the valuing and diagnostic steps (Steps 2 and 3) of Web Business Engineering.

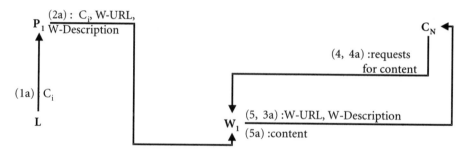

Figure 13-17. *The brokered, direct marketing approach*

Step 4: Treat Business

Although the producer can't beam W's information directly into the user's head, maybe it's possible for W to push the Web site's description and information into C's head (see Figure 13-18).

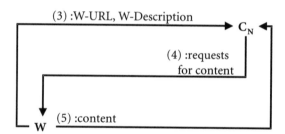

Figure 13-18. *Our goal: Web site direct marketing*

One treatment we can try is to substitute W for both brokers in our passive-brokered and proactive-brokered maps (see Figures 13-15 and 13-16). This substitution amounts to having W take on all the responsibilities (content) of B (see Figure 13-19).

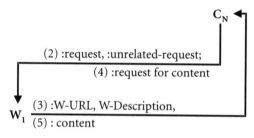

Figure 13-19. *W playing both passive and proactive roles*

The problem with this treatment is that it makes no sense. If C is already at W, then there is really no reason to push W's URL and description on C. A better alternative is for P to create a separate secondary Web site (W_p) and use that Web site to substitute for the broker, B (see Figure 13-20). One implementation is to build a search engine on W_p that always ranks P's Web site (W_1) at the top and have newsgroups and chat rooms on W_p that automatically advertise W_1's URL and description. P still has the problem of generating a large amount traffic to W_p in order for this treatment to work, but if P is able to grow W_p or P buys an existing broker, then this treatment is a good one.

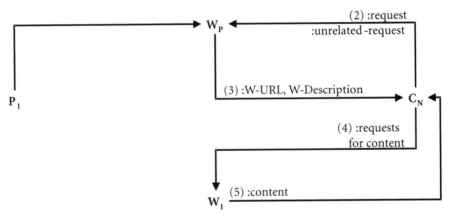

Figure 13-20. *Creating a secondary Web business for the primary one (W_1) to serve as a broker*

However, let's assume that P cannot create another Web site. P must use existing mechanisms in addition to whatever P can come up with. Is there anything P can do to generate traffic? Our final way is the least expensive method of generating traffic and is based on the brokered direct marketing activity map (Figure 13–17). Instead of the content provider (P) manually generating leads (C_i), the customers themselves (C) generate them. Such an activity is an example of a *recursive mechanism* for generating traffic, so named because the members of the target community—your customers—call on themselves to bring traffic to P's Web site.

The benefit of this approach is that it costs (P) nothing to generate leads except for the initial costs of developing the recursive mechanism. Moreover, if one implements the recursion correctly, instead of one customer providing one lead, a single customer can provide multiple leads. In theory, the Web site's traffic should grow exponentially. However, there are several potential problems with such a mechanism. First, it assumes the customer will enter valid leads. Second, even if the customer does enter valid leads, there is no guarantee that the leads will come to W.

In this next chapter we use Web Business Engineering to help us develop the foundation for a theory on *Memetic Marketing*, which will help us overcome some of these problems.

CHAPTER FOURTEEN

Fundamentals of Memetic Marketing

Executive Summary

The information analogy of a gene is a *meme,* a kind of information pattern that travels from person to person throughout a culture. Because most Web businesses are information intensive, one can usefully view any online business as a collection of memes. In this chapter we build a theory of marketing Web businesses based on the idea of a Web business as a collection of memes. Not all memes in a Web site are equal in terms of distribution (or replication) potential. First, we'll examine what makes a good Web meme. A good Web meme represents a computational instrument on your site that provides work, social, or intellectual currency— content that can be put to good use in work, social, or intellectual situations. Having characterized a good Web meme, we then examine what it takes to spread this meme. We show that the word-of-mouth method has limitations that technology can overcome. We will see that any technological solution for replicating memes requires that the content provider design three types of incentives: referral, viewing, and visiting. With the proper incentives built into the replication mechanism, content providers can realize order of magnitude response rates over traditional direct-marketing techniques. Finally, we will analyze an actual example of a successful meme and its Web-based replication mechanism.

Objectives

After reading this chapter you should be able to

- *Explain what constitutes a good meme*

- *Design an effective replication mechanism for a business Web site*

Introduction

What survives from one family generation to the next? The answer: family genes. While family members can look very different because of genes, the genes themselves are similar, and get passed down from one generation to the next. So imagine that people really aren't important. Pretend what's really important are the genes, and people are just devices that genes created (through biological evolution) to spread themselves. In 1976, Richard Dawkins wrote the book *Selfish Gene,* which promotes this concept. However, what's even more interesting and thought-provoking is that Dawkins extended this view to information. He called the information equivalent of a gene a meme, and people, along with the technologies they used, were the devices that information "created" (through cultural evolution) to replicate itself.

Religion is the classic example of a meme. It is information that spreads from person to person and generation to generation within a culture through a combination of word of mouth and technologies (such as books). More modern examples of memes can be found in television and radio commercials. For example, how often have we (in the United States)—said, "Just do it!"—the phrase from Nike's television commercial? And how many of us can hum the tune to Oscar Mayer's hotdog jingle: "Oh, I wish I were an Oscar Mayer Wiener . . ." Both phrase and song, respectively, are examples of memes that have spread throughout our culture.

Of course, not all information spreads in this manner, just certain kinds of information. This information is often deemed "catchy," although catchy is never precisely defined. Nevertheless, the meme concept is a useful one because a Web site, when reduced to its basic components, is simply a collection of information and computations. If content providers can identify what constitutes the valuable content on a Web site and then associate the Web business's address with a catchy description of this content, they can more effectively spread information from their online business as well as the information necessary to drive traffic to it. And, hopefully, content providers can use technology to aid in the widespread and rapid distribution of this information—replicating the memes.

This chapter builds a theory of marketing based on the meme concept. We will examine what makes for a good meme in a Web business and the limitations of word of mouth in spreading, or replicating, memes. We then use Web Business Engineering to identify ways to use the online technologies to aid in the replication process. We will see a successful Web business meme and its replication mechanism, which was built according to the principles outlined in this chapter.

What Content Makes a Good Web Meme?

For our purposes let's define a Web meme as a description or *representation* of your Web site or something on your Web site that spreads from user to user. To help us understand what makes a good Web meme, suppose you have a fortune-telling Web site, *www.yesnomaybe.com.* Ideally, you'd like just the Web site's address to be the meme that spreads from person to person (see Figure 14-1). But people probably aren't willing to spread just the site's address because by itself it's useless. An effective meme has to also describe content on your site that people find valuable—such content is considered valuable when it has social, work, everyday, or entertainment purposes. A Web site's address is merely a pointer to a place where people can get valuable content; it's not the value itself. So, typically by itself, the Web site address is not a good meme.

But if people had an idea of the value the site would provide, this information coupled with the site's address might spread from person to person, *assuming* the value was high enough and described adequately. Therefore a good Web meme ought to include a site's address and a description of the value people will get from the site (Figure 14-2). Now a general description of the value users can expect from a site—fortune-telling—is a good start, but it's not the kind of description that will make a person immediately want to tell a friend.

:www.yesnomaybe.com

Figure 14-1. *An incomplete meme: the Web site address*

:www.yesnomaybe.com, fortune-telling

Figure 14-2. *A more complete meme: the Web site address and a description of the value people will get from the site*

One way content providers can improve the chances of spreading their Web meme is by being more specific about the value users will get from visiting their site—by describing only a single or small number of key content areas that users will find interesting enough to tell their friends about. This task is not as simple as it seems. A Web site typically contains many different kinds of information that users may find valuable. However, we can trim down the possibilities by adding several constraints on the content, one of which is that it generates return visits. As content providers, we want the same people to visit our Web site many times. Interesting or entertaining static information, like yearly doom predictions, may get people to visit, and they may even tell their friends what they read about, but once read and spread, there is no incentive for that person *or* their friends to come back to the Web site. So interesting and entertaining static information may make for a good meme but not a good Web meme.

The content described by a Web meme must contain *dynamic* content, information that changes either on a regular basis—because the Web master adds new content—or, even better, changes in response to user information (see Figure 14-3). An example of the former would be a weekly doom predictor that predicts what the next big catastrophe is and when it will occur, based on current world events. The content is interesting enough that people will want to tell their friends about it, and, because the content changes, people and their friends will return to the site for more.

:www.yesnomaybe.com, weekly doom predictions

Figure 14-3.   *A better meme, which describes dynamic content*

Now for meme purposes, having content providers dynamically vary content is better than static content, but an even better alternative is to have users vary their own content. Sticking with our doom prediction example, imagine that instead of a weekly doom predictor, there was a doom predictor that forecasted the possibility of success or doom in response to a user-described situation (see Figure 14-4). Not only is such a doom predictor more dynamic than a weekly doom predictor, it has the added benefit of providing *personalized* content and therefore higher value, on the average, than content added by a Web master.

> ## :www.yesnomaybe.com, personal doom predictions

Figure 14-4.   *An even better meme, which describes dynamic,*
personalized content

To summarize, a good Web meme should include (1) the Web site's address and (2) a description of valuable content on the site, where content is deemed valuable if it is entertaining or if it provides information that can be used in social or work situations; and (3), the content should vary dynamically and be customized by the user. Now that we know what makes a good Web meme, let's now look at how to spread such a meme.

How a Meme Spreads Without Technology

In the absence of technology, a meme spreads from person to person within a culture through word of mouth. In the ideal case, the meme spreads quickly to every person in the culture. At least four factors determine the speed and extent to which a meme spreads. The first is *latency:* the time that elapses between when a person first hears about a meme to the time when that person tells someone else about it. Suppose the meme is a good joke. An example of a short latency would be when a person, upon hearing a meme, immediately gets on the phone and tells a friend about it. An example of a long latency would be that same person waiting for the next party to tell a friend about it.

This last example highlights the second factor that determines how fast a meme spreads: *context.* In order for one person to tell another person about something, he or she needs to be in a situation or context where it is appropriate to say it. Suppose the meme being spread is the address of an auction Web site. This meme is likely to come up in situations where the conversation centers on finding the best price for a product or in conversations about a product one of them just bought. If the conversation topic never shifts to one where it's appropriate to mention the meme, it may never come up.

To this point, we've been primarily discussing situations where one person tells another person about a meme (see Figure 14-5), who, we hope, then tells another person, and so on. However, even if one could somehow create the proper contexts and minimize latencies, it may take a while for a meme to spread, particularly if the number of users in a culture is small. For this reason, another factor becomes important: *fan-out.*

$$C_1 \longrightarrow C_2 \longrightarrow \cdots \longrightarrow C_N$$

Figure 14-5.   *One-to-one spread*

Fan-out is the number of people to which a given person spreads a meme (see Figure 14-6). Suppose a person tells two people about a meme. These two people then tell two other people about the meme, and so on. Latencies being equal, it is clear that this kind of multiperson spreading is faster than the one-to-one person spread. The higher the fan-out, the faster the meme spreads throughout the culture.

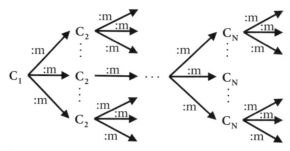

Figure 14-6.   *A one-person to many-persons spread*

The fourth factor that determines the spread of the meme is *accuracy.* For a meme to spread, it must be accurately communicated from one individual to another. For example, pretend the meme is a good joke. Suppose the person that knows the joke starts to tell a friend but forgets the punch line. It is unlikely that the friend will then tell the same joke to someone else. The meme's spreading stops at that instant and only continues because, hopefully, there are other individuals who can accurately remember all of the joke when communicating it.

These are some of the problems when people serve as meme replicators. What are the benefits? The primary benefit is that if a friend tells one or more friends, the chances are that those friends will do the same. The reason is that friends are usually individuals with similar interests. So if the meme is interesting to one friend, it's likely that it will spread to all of his or her friends as well.

Our design goals are to find ways to use online technologies in such a manner that the proper contexts are created for accurately spreading our memes while minimizing latencies and maximizing fan-outs.

Using the Web to Replicate a Meme

Assume a customer (C) visits a content provider's (P) Web site (W) (refer to Steps 1 and 2 in Figure 14-7). Further assume that the meme P wants to spread is W's URL, along with a description of some valuable content area(s) in W. In the absence of help from technology, the meme spreads via C telling friends (C_i's) about it (see Step 3, Figure 14-7). The friends then visit W and, hopefully, spread the meme in a similar fashion.

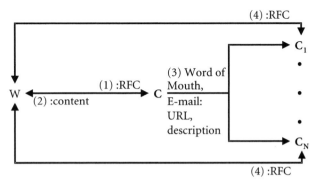

Figure 14-7. *People as replicators, no technology assistance.*

One clear problem with this model is that P has no control over the context, latency, fan-out, or accuracy factors that affect meme replication. So it may take a while for situations to arise where C tells his or her friends (C_is) about the meme—and who's to say that C *will* tell all of his or her friends? And even assuming C does tell many friends, C may still forget meme details such as W's address. So P must hope the quality of W's memes are high enough that they spread quickly and abundantly in P's target market.

One way to get around these problems is for P to provide C with some kind of *referral incentive* to spread the word to friends (see Figure 14-8). For example, P can pay C some amount of money for each friend that visits. If the amount is high enough, this kind of referral incentive solves the context, latency, and fan-out problems. However, there is still the potential of C communicating the information incorrectly. Another problem is that this referral model can get expensive. Finally, the meme may be communicated, but it may take the C_is a while to visit the Web site. Perhaps there is a way to use online technologies, specifically W itself, to solve these problems.

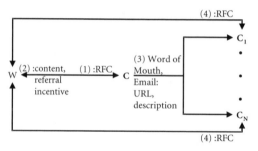

Figure 14-8.   *Adding incentives to ensure information spreading*

Instead of having C relay the meme (URL, description) to friends (C$_i$s), W can do it. Using Web Business Engineering, we simply distribute the meme so that W delivers it instead of C (see Figure 14-9, Step 4). Unfortunately, W does not know who C's friends are.

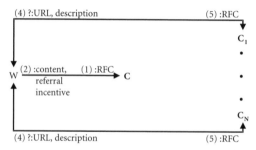

Figure 14-9.   *First attempt at Web Business as replicator*

So, W must first retrieve contact information from C (:C$_i$, Figure 14-10). The same referral incentive used to get C to tell friends about W (Step 2) can be used to get C to tell W about his or her friends (Step 3). The contact information can be as simple as an e-mail address. With the e-mail address stored in some database, W can then immediately deliver the meme to C's friends (Step 4).

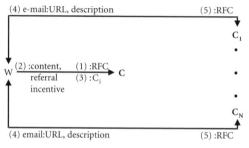

Figure 14-10.   *Web site as meme replicator*

E-mail isn't the only vehicle W can use to deliver the meme to C's friends. P can shorten the latency even further by using a technology like instant messaging (IM) to deliver the meme to C's friends (see Figure 14-11, Step 4).

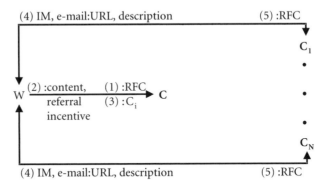

Figure 14-11. *Faster Web site qua meme replicator*

However, spreading the meme over e-mail only solves part of the problem. There is still the problem of getting C's friends to actually visit the Web site (see Figure 14-12, Step 5). To solve this problem it is necessary for P to provide a visiting incentive alongside the meme (see Step 4).

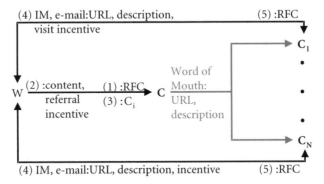

Figure 14-12. *Adding visiting incentives*

Finally, depending on the medium, it may also be necessary for P to provide a viewing incentive to C's friends (see Figure 14-13, Step 4). In our example, this would be an incentive to read the e-mail or to read the IM message, without which the user would not visit the Web site to start the replication process all over again.

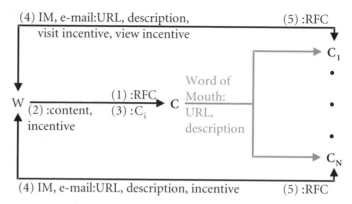

Figure 14-13. *Adding view incentives*

In summary, creating a good meme replicator for a Web business first requires a mass-contact mechanism such as e-mail, instant messaging, or a newsgroup. Along with a mass-contact mechanism, the content provider needs to design at least three types of incentives. The first is a *referral incentive*. This is an incentive P provides C in order to get contact information (C_i). The second incentive is a *viewing incentive*. This is an incentive to get C_i to view the message (at all!). The third incentive is a *visiting incentive*. This is an incentive to get C_i to go to the Web business. In the next section we examine an actual Web example of a meme replicator.

Example: A Good Web Meme and Web Replicator

A good Web replicator starts with a good Web meme. The meme in the Dating Expert Web site is a "love compatibility" calculator. Briefly, the way it works is that a customer enters two names, typically his or her name and the name of another person—presumably a person that he or she likes. The love compatibility calculator then computes their compatibility along love, sexual, and intellectual dimensions (see Figure 14-14). Now this kind of mechanism makes a good meme because it provides information that people not only *can* but *want* to share with one another—social currency. However, as stated in the previous sections, having a good meme is not enough. The meme needs a replicator, and if one is using the Web as the replication mechanism, several incentives need to be implemented.

Reality The Dating Expert Meme Replicator gets a 13 to 14 percent response rate, an order of magnitude higher than "offline" mass-mailing programs (1 percent), and two orders of magnitude higher than e-mail spam (0.1 percent).

Referral Incentive

The love compatibility calculator provides value in the form of social currency. As such, there is already a "natural" desire to share this information with other people. The referral mechanism simply has to be built into the love calculator. The next kind of incentive is a viewing incentive.

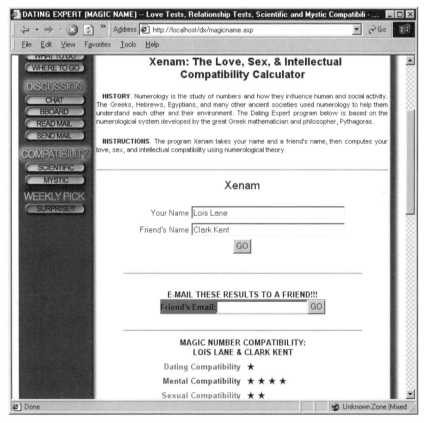

Figure 14-14.   *The meme—a love compatibility calculator*

Viewing Incentive

The results of the love compatibility test are e-mailed to the person the test-taker specified, usually a friend. However, with all the e-mail spam people receive, unless the e-mail is "From:" a friend or acquaintance, the receiver may not read it at all. For e-mail, it goes without saying that the best viewing incentive is to doctor the message so that it appears to come from a friend or acquaintance. In a mailing program, this would look like Figure 14-15.

From	Date	Subject
Nancy	4/10/99	Check this out Nick

Figure 14-15.　*E-mail with "From:" line doctored to contain the name of a friend*

Doctoring "From:" this way is possible because Dating Expert customers have to register to use the site's free services, and the registration process includes the customer entering their e-mail. However, for privacy reasons—the person sending the e-mail may not want the receiver to know who they are—the e-mail has to be sent anonymously.

Thus, with e-mail the only (viable) place left to add a visiting incentive is the subject line. But not just any old message will work. For example, a common e-mail spam subject is the one shown in Figure 14-16, a simple "Hi!"

From	Date	Subject
Unknown	4/10/99	Hi!

Figure 14-16.　*An ineffective viewing incentive*

What's good about the subject line is that it plays to a person's sense of curiosity. And prior to the online public's awareness of spam, it was probably a good message. However, too many spammers have used this as a subject, and people are likely to ignore such e-mails. So, we seem to be at an impasse. People won't read e-mails unless they're from a friend, but we have to send an e-mail anonymously. The solution is to send an anonymous e-mail from the next best thing to a friend, and, in the case of Dating Expert, the "next best thing" is a secret admirer (see Figure 14-17).

The subject line in Figure 14-17 piques a person's curiosity the same way the "Hi!" message does, but it has the added bonus of indicating that the message comes from a person who likes them (and who can resist an e-mail from an admirer?). Now that you've gotten the person to read the e-mail, the next goal is to get that person to visit the Web site.

> **Subject:** Your Secret Admirer Says Hi!

Figure 14-17. *Dating Expert viewing incentive*

Visit Incentive

Quite simply, the goal in creating an effective visiting incentive is to design an e-mail message that makes the recipient *want* to visit. The Dating Expert Web site accomplishes this in four ways. First, the e-mail provides a clear sense of the value the recipient will receive if he or she visits the Dating Expert Web site, namely compatibility tests. Specifically, the e-mail contains the compatibility test results between two people, one of which is presumably the recipient but both of whom the recipient probably knows. So, the e-mail is both *customized* and *relevant* to the recipient. The test results are a form of social currency, information that the recipient can use in (later) social situations. For example, this information can be used as an excuse to contact the individuals mentioned in the compatibility test or as the discussion topic at a party, to name just a few social uses. Note, however, that the e-mail contains the test results but not an explanation of what the results mean. To get this explanation, the recipient needs to visit the Dating Expert Web site. Thus, the e-mail provides *incomplete* information that must be combined with information found at the Web site. Finally, the e-mail makes it easy for the recipient to visit by placing hyperlinks at the top and the bottom of the message (see Figure 14-18).

'Your Secret Admirer' ran the "Love, Brainz, and Sexual Compatibility" Test for you at http://www.datingexpert.com/magicnames.asp !!!

The compatibility results for the couple 'Clark Kent' – 'Lois Lane' are:

Dating Score: ****
Mental Score: ****
Sexual Score: ****

*****Visit http://www.datingexpert.com/magicnames.asp for a detailed explanation of the scores!!! *****

Figure 14-18. *E-mail content, visiting incentive*

In summary, the key to creating a good e-mail visiting incentive is to provide a clear sense of the value the recipients will receive, while making the information relevant, albeit incomplete, to the user and making it easy to visit the Web site by providing hypertext links in the message. Having instrumented our site to attract customers, let's use Web Business Engineering to make money off of them.

CHAPTER FIFTEEN

Issues in Revenue Generation for Information-Based Web Businesses

Executive Summary

Suppose you have used Web Business Engineering (WBE) to develop a high-value-added, information-based Web business and have also implemented the necessary mechanisms for generating traffic. Now you must decide what to charge for your services. It is a good idea to bill (1) at *value-endpoints,* points in your online activities where the user has extracted value and could otherwise leave without paying, and (2) for *information transactions,* that provide high value at low risk. But money isn't the only form of payment. This chapter presents a payment model that argues for payment in terms of *information-currency* or *I-currency*—information that other businesses value and are willing to pay money for—depending on an information transaction's value-to-risk ratio. You charge different I-payments based on your content's value-risk ratio. Finally, we will discuss how to seamlessly integrate payment into a Web business's activities.

Objectives

After reading this chapter you should be able to:

■ *Explain the concept of an information transaction*

■ *Define information currency*

■ *Decide what content on your site you can charge users to access*

■ *Determine the best form of payment for the different kinds of content on your site*

Introduction

Suppose you have used Web Business Engineering to create a Web business with high-value-added and good traffic-generating mechanisms. Although you are way ahead of most other Web businesses, there is still one step remaining if you're going to have a successful online presence—instrumenting your Web business to receive proper payment for the value you're providing.

Online payment is not as simple as offline payment for a variety of reasons. For example, when paying for goods in an offline, brick-and-mortar business, there is usually a designated area for payment. Furthermore, because customers are getting a tangible product that they are probably familiar with, they have a fairly good idea of what they are paying for and why it's worth that much.

In contrast, in a Web business each information transaction—a request for content (:RFC) by one agent that results in a response (:content) by another agent (see Figure 15-1)—between a consumer and the Web business is a potential payment point.

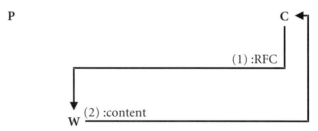

Figure 15-1. *An information transaction*

Ideally, as a content provider, you'd like to charge a customer for each information transaction (see Figure 15-2), that amounts to a *pay-per-content* model.

Each time a customer (C) requests content (:RFC, Step 1), the Web site (W) first requests payment (:RFP, Step 2). Only if C pays (:payment, Step 3) does W deliver the content requested (:content, Step 4). However, this scenario typically isn't practical for several reasons. Since the good being delivered is information and not a tangible product, customers may not have a good sense of the value they're receiving and may be unwilling to pay. Second, if the value is too small, customers may be resistant to making micropayments. Finally, there may be other Web businesses where users can get the same information for free.

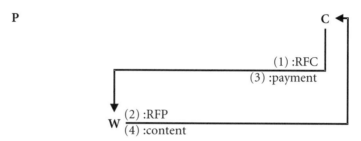

Figure 15-2. *Pay-per-content model*

A straightforward "tweak" to the pay-per-content model is to have the customer only pay for *valuable* content (see Figure 15-3). However, the pay-per-valuable-content model raises two important issues: What qualifies as valuable content? What "currency" do customers pay us with?

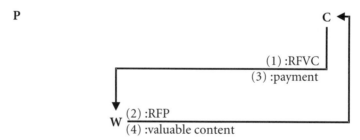

Figure 15-3. *Pay-per-valuable-content model*

To help resolve these issues, let's take an actual example of a complex online activity with many steps, or information transactions: the Dating Expert matchmaking activity. Although the activity we're examining is specific to a particular domain, the results generalize to any online activity consisting of a number of information transactions. The analysis begins with the business activity maps you (should have) created when you initially designed your Web business.

Case Study: Dating Expert Matchmaking Activity

The Dating Expert matchmaking activity (see Figure 15-4) consists of 13 steps. C first makes a request to search W's personal ads—by clicking on W's matchmaking link (Step 1). W returns a search form to C, which allows C to specify what kind of date he or she is looking for (Step 2). C uses the form to send his or her search criteria to W (Step 3), who returns a list of names that fit C's search criteria (Step 4). C can then read the personal ad by clicking on the person's name (Step 5). W returns the potential date's (D) personal ad (Step 6). C can then contact any potential date (D) by sending a message to his or her private mailbox (Step 7). Such messages usually contain more detailed information about C along with a request to either: (1) contact C outside of the Web site—via e-mail, phone, or through various instant message programs—or (2) to provide C with D's contact information (Steps 8 to 10). If D responds, then C can read the contact information from his or her private mailbox (Steps 11 and 12) and contact D outside of W (Step 13).

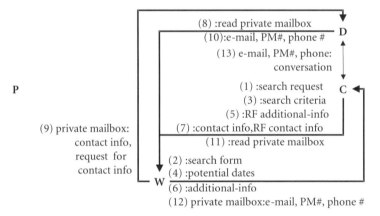

Figure 15-4.   *The matchmaking activity (free model)*

Note that if C and D get to Step 13 without your extracting some form of payment, then in essence they have "left" your Web business without paying! Clearly we need to extract some payment before they leave. As mentioned, each *information transaction* is a candidate for payment. Focusing on C, there are six information transactions that one can potentially charge for: four between C and W (1, 2), (3, 4), (5, 6), and (11, 12); one directly between C and D (13); and one between C and D, mediated by W (7–10). There is also an information transaction between D and W (8, 9).

Different Places to Charge—the Big Issues

Let's examine these different places in the matchmaking activity where we can charge the customer, noting ways of charging as well as trying to understand whether it is indeed a good place to charge the customer.

Charging to Initiate a Search. First, the content provider (P) can charge C for initiating a search (Figure 15-5). There are many different ways to implement this payment mechanism. At the extremes, C can pay just once and perform as many searches as desired, or C can pay for each search request.

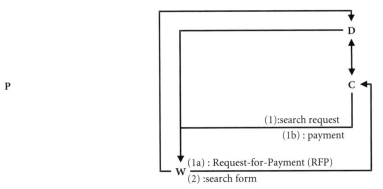

Figure 15-5. *Pay to search*

The problem is that P is charging C at the beginning of the activity, where C does not have a clear idea of what he or she is getting, if anything. If P has many competitors whose Web sites promise similar content at little or no cost, then P risks turning customers away. In short, from C's perspective, this is a point in the activity with uncertain (high-risk) value. If P insists on asking for payment, it must be a small enough amount that C doesn't simply switch to a competitor's Web site. Fortunately, charging at the beginning of the matchmaking activity isn't the only place to charge.

Charging for Smart Searches. Conventional wisdom suggests charging for services that your Web site provides that offer more value compared to similar offline or competitors' services. For example, online matchmaking services provide value over other (offline) forms of matchmaking, like newspaper personal ads, by giving the date seeker more flexible search capabilities. P can charge for this added-value mechanism (see Figure 15-6). One way to implement this mechanism is to provide a search form that allows basic search capabilities for free—say, free searches on broad categories like location and age—but charges C for searching on more specific categories like interests and religion, criteria that C can't easily search for using offline matchmaking services.

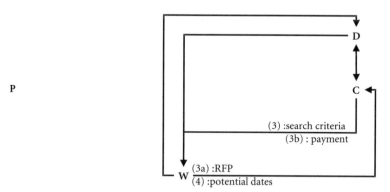

Figure 15-6. *Pay for smart searches*

It should be noted that for search results, the Dating Expert Web site returns a list of names along with a compatibility score and astrological sign, not the entire personal ad (see Figure 12-20 in Chapter 12). Now the problem with charging for searches is that there is no guarantee that the searches will return any names. One way around this problem is to charge a fee for each name returned. Unfortunately, if the search returns thousands of names, for example, C will have to pay a large sum and may be unwilling to do so. And even if there was a way to restrict the search results to a small number, C still runs the risk of not finding a good match after actually viewing the personal ads. Thus, from C's perspective, there is still high risk and potentially low return at this step in the activity, albeit lower and higher risk/return, respectively, compared to the previous step. The next step, charging for reading the personal ads, provides lower risk and higher value and may be a better place to charge.

Charging to Read Personal Ads. The Dating Expert Web site returns a list of potential dates, along with a compatibility ranking, similar to how a Web search engine returns an ordered list of Web sites. Implemented in this manner, C must click on a potential date's name to read his or her personal ad, which allows P to charge C prior to reading an ad (Figure 15-7). Similar to paying for searches, C can either pay once, reading as many personal ads as desired, or C can pay per personal ad.

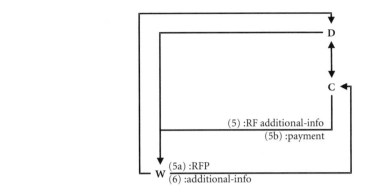

Figure 15-7. *Pay to read personal ads*

However, reading a personal ad is not a guarantee that C is going to find a good match, for a number of reasons. The person that placed the ad may have lied or omitted a detail (such as being a smoker) that doesn't get filtered out in the search activity and that makes the person incompatible with C. So from C's perspective there is the risk that even after reading the personal ad, there is a chance of not finding a match. Thus, C may not be willing to pay or only willing to pay a small amount for the privilege of reading personal ads. It seems like the best place to charge C is when C finds a personal ad that he or she likes. We can operationalize what it means to find a good personal ad in the next step.

Charging to Contact. If C finds a good potential date (D), C must establish contact. For privacy and security reasons, Dating Expert has been set up so that C can only contact D by sending mail to D's private mailbox, which is hosted on W. Note, however, that because the private mailboxes are hosted on W, P can charge C for sending mail to D (see Figure 15-8).

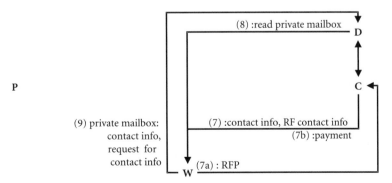

Figure 15-8. *Pay to forward information*

Charging P to contact D seems like a good idea for two reasons. First, the Web site has provided C with something he or she wants. Second, it makes sense to charge at this point because the customers may exchange information like phone numbers or e-mails that would allow them to interact outside of the Dating Expert Web site. If so, the customers will have "left without paying." This point in the activity is a *value-endpoint,* a point in the activity where C has an explicit idea of the value W is providing, as well as the point at which C can leave without paying! Thus, at the very least the information transactions that ought to be charged for are those at value endpoints. Are there other value endpoints in the Dating Expert matchmaking activity?

Charging to Read Private Mailboxes. One can define a match as occurring when D contacts C. The contact is "made" when C reads his or her private mailbox (Figure 15-9). Note, however, there are in fact two areas where contact is made: when D reads his or her mailbox (Step 8) and when C reads C's private mailbox (Step 11)—two places where P can charge for reading messages.

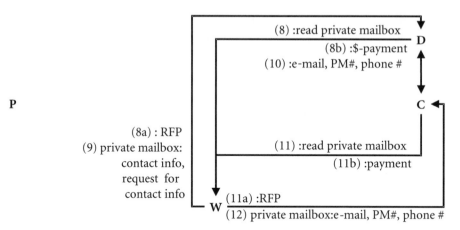

Figure 15-9.   *Pay to read private mailbox*

Paying to read e-mail seems like an even better idea than paying to establish contact. Both C and D know that the other person is interested, and the probability of a match and further contact is high, even higher than the previous step. Because both C and D have a good idea of what they're getting, reading mail is a value endpoint. Also note that if you do not charge C and D to read e-mail, they can "leave without paying," which is consistent with our definition of a value endpoint.

In short, at this step in the activity, which is also a value endpoint, C and D receive the maximum value with the lowest risk. Thus, this is the best place to charge the customer for the value Dating Expert provides.

Deciding What to Charge For: High Value, Low Risk

The general rule of thumb when deciding what to charge for is pay-per-value. However, it is clear from our analysis that value needs to be weighted by risk. More precisely, when deciding what to charge for in one's Web businesses, the better heuristic is to ask for payment at those steps in your online activities with low risk and high value, as well as areas where customers have received value and could leave the Web site without paying. The latter condition is necessary because there may be steps in your online activities with higher value-to-risk ratio, but they occur after steps in the activity where the user can "leave without paying."

To systematically determine what to charge for, content providers ought to list the information transactions on their Web site, along with an assessment of their relative risks and value from the customer's perspective. The value of an information transaction can be determined in a number of ways. For example, a trial run of the Web business can be performed and the number of page hits recorded. Those pages with a high number of hits are associated with high value information transactions. Risk is more difficult to quantify, but it can be determined by user studies, focus groups, and surveys. However, in the absence of actual numbers for value and risk, the assessment can be qualitative, where value and risk are ranked as either low, moderate, or high (see Figure 15-10), or one can assign a numeric ranking to the information transactions.

Information Transformation	Value	Risk	Charge Money?
1	LOW	HIGH	NO
2	LOW	HIGH	NO
3	MOD	MOD	NO
4	HIGH	LOW	YES
5	HIGH	LOW	YES

Figure 15-10. *Sample value-risk table*

Those information transactions with low risk and high value are the ones that content providers can charge money for. But what about information transactions with lower value and higher risk, low value and low risk, or high value and high risk? Are those free of charge? The short answer is no. Customers may be unwilling to pay money for risky information transactions, but they may be able to pay other forms of currency that content providers can later transform into money. Let's look at such nonmonetary payments, or what I call *information currency*.

Information Currency

Up to this point we've assumed that charging the customer meant that the customer had to pay the content provider money. But that isn't necessarily the case. Information is money, and nowhere is this truer than in today's information-intensive, online world. The Web makes it relatively easy to collect consumer information, *and* there are certain kinds of information that content providers can sell to businesses in exchange for money. I define any information that can be exchanged for money as information currency, or *I-currency*. For example, a Web business can collect customer addresses and demographics, then sell this information to businesses that collect mailing lists. Offline businesses have been doing this for years. The online equivalent to selling mailing addresses is selling leads. There are businesses such as *Visto.com* that will pay content providers for their customers' information, which can be delivered simply by redirecting customers to a registration link on the business's Web site. Such businesses ask for address, e-mail, and other demographics and contact information. The content provider typically gets from $1 to $3 for each customer, or "lead," delivered. It shouldn't be too long before businesses start charging for more immediate contact information such as "instant messaging" addresses.

I-currency varies in terms of how easy it is to liquidate. An example of I-currency that is relatively difficult to liquidate is the address and demographics information, where content providers must collect a large number of such information before they can sell it. I-currencies that are easy to liquidate are e-mail addresses and other contact information, since there are companies that will pay for each lead delivered.

I-currency is important for online businesses because, while customers may be unwilling to pay money for information transactions with high risk, they may be willing to pay for such high-risk transactions with "low-cost" currency, a.k.a. information currency. Information currency is low cost because it costs the customer virtually nothing to provide it except for the customer's time. Using

I-currency, content providers can charge for any information transactions that are high value since charging I-currency effectively lowers the risk from the customer's point of view. The only information transaction that a content provider *shouldn't* charge for are those where the information is of low value and high risk. All other information transactions should require some form of payment from the customer, either monetary or an I-payment. The different forms of payment are summarized in Figure 15-11.

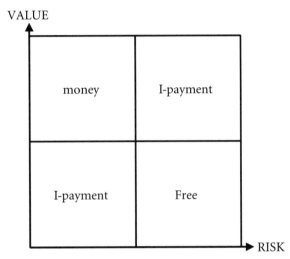

Figure 15-11. *Value-risk payment chart*

When designing online activities, the ultimate goal is for all information transactions to lie in the upper left quadrant: low risk, high value. However, this diagram can help guide the redesign of existing Web businesses. Given an information transaction, first locate where on the value-risk payment chart your site's information transactions lie. Charge for these transactions accordingly. Next, use Web Business Engineering to redesign the site's online activities, so that the new information transactions lie in the low-risk, high-value quadrant (see Figure 15-12).

For example, suppose you are designing an employment Web site where one of the links is to a Web page that contains static interview tips. A look at the traffic to the Web site shows that this link has received very few hits and is therefore of little value; this link is in the lower left corner of the chart. After applying Web Business Engineering, you decide that an *interactive* mock-interview Web page is needed, where the user can engage the Web site in a simulated interview. You've increased the value of that particular link, or information transaction, so at the very least that part of your site is in the upper right quadrant; high value, high risk. Your next task is to reduce the consumer's perceived risk in accessing this link. One way to do this is to collect statistics showing that users who access your mock-interview link have a high success rate during interviews. You then publish these statistics on your site. You've now not only increased the value of the information transactions associated with the interview link, but you've also lowered the user's perceived risk in paying for this value. Thus, you can charge money for this link or, worst case, an I-payment.

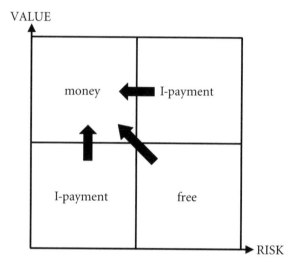

Figure 15-12.   *Using the value-risk chart to guide design and redesign*

Conclusion

By using Web business engineering to increase the value of the content areas in your Web business and charging the appropriate payment, you will optomize your site's revenue. I like to think of Web consultants, Web entrepreneurs, and Web designers in general, as musicians of sorts. But instead of playing music you can hear, they play music you can interact with: a Web site. Web Business Engineering, then, is simply a style in the same way that jazz, blues, and rock & roll are musical styles. My intent in creating Web Business Engineering is not to make Web design a science but rather to impose a structure that you can work with to make the kind of music that businesses like to hear. I hope you will enjoy creating your "music" in this style.

Bibliography

Alter, S. *Information Systems: A Management Perspective.* Menlo Park, CA: Benjamin/ Cummings, 1996.

Bartholomew, D. "Clinging to EDI," *Industry Week*, 246, 6-23-1997, p. 44.

Davenport, T. H. *Process Improvement: Reengineering Work Through Information Technology.* Boston, MA: HBS Press, 1993.

Dawkins, R. *The Selfish Gene.* Oxford: Oxford University Press, 1976.

Flor, N., and P. Maglio. "Modeling Business Representational Activity Online: A Case Study." Proceedings of the 1997 International Conference in Information Systems.

Flor, N., and P. Maglio. "Global Control of Local Activity" Proceedings of the 1997 International Conference on Computer Support for Collaborative Learning.

Harrington, H. J. *Business Process Improvement.* New York, NY: McGraw-Hill, 1991.

Hutchins, E. *Cognition in the Wild.* Cambridge, MA: Bradford Books: MIT Press, 1995.

Mullaney, T. "Business Week e.biz: Clicks & Misses: Online Shopping Bargaining Power," *Business Week*, 3658, 12-13-1999, p. 90.

Tully, S. "Features/The Auction Economy: Going, Going, Gone! The B2B Tool That Really Is Changing the World," *Fortune*, 3-30-2000, pp. 132+.

Wilder, C., and J. Gambon. "The New Groupware Dynamic—As Netscape Aims to Make Collaborative Computing Affordable, Lotus and Others Ready Their Own Offerings," *Information Week*, 10-21-1996, p. 14.

Index